NORWEGIAN ROSEMALING

Painted from floor to ridge beam in the early 1800's by Telemark artist Ola Hansson, this room is part of a home in the outdoor museum at Skien, Norway. Copyright: © *Photos Norge*

NORWEGIAN ROSEMALING

Decorative Painting on Wood

Margaret M. Miller and
Sigmund Aarseth

Charles Scribner's Sons / New York

To the Rosemaling Masters
Who Developed the Style and
Carried the Tradition Through the Years

3 5 7 9 11 13 15 17 19   C/M   20 18 16 14 12 10 8 6 4 2

Printed in the United States of America
Library of Congress Catalog Card Number 72-495
SBN 684-12943-4 (cloth)

ACKNOWLEDGMENTS

THE GREATEST PLEASURE in completing work on a book comes from being able to express gratitude to those that gave generously of their time and creative abilities in assisting with the finished work.

The authors are fortunate in having many friends on both sides of the Atlantic to thank. Firstly, we wish to acknowledge those living in Norway, the homeland of rosemaling.

A special thanks to Sigmund's dear and patient wife, Ingebjorg, for helping, not only with the book but with all his projects and travels; and to Kolbein Dahle who put a tremendous amount of effort into the photographs both of old rosemaling and of old buildings. Many of these he either found and selected or took himself. He also photographed Sigmund painting for all of the technical photographs of brush strokes. Several Norwegian rosemaling masters: Ruth Nordbø, wife of Gunnar Nordbø; Knut Andersen of Porsgrunn Porcelain; Bergljot Lunde, teacher in the craftschool at Sand, Norway; and Lars Sataøyen, Hallingdal rosemaler, all courteously allowed photos of their work to be included. Nils Ellingsgard, a Hallingdal master whose work appears in many photos, generously helped correct the chapters on "Color" and "Brush Strokes" and provided several of the special illustrations on Hallingdal strokes. Halvor Landsverk, Director of the folkemuseum at Skien and Per Hvamstad, Director of the Valdres Folkemuseum, gave technical assistance and provided and authenticated many photos.

Secondly, in rosemaling's adopted homeland, the United States, our debts of gratitude are especially deep to two people who did more to help on the book than any others. They are: Dean E. Madden of Decatur, Ill. and Mrs. Gerhard Miller of Sturgeon Bay, Wis. Dean Madden, the moving genius behind so many Norwegian art projects in the U.S., not only personally photographed and provided a great number of photographs (which are credited in the book as © Photos Norge) but lent his ideas and organizational skills to all aspects of this project. Mr. and Mrs. Gerhard Miller both gave constant support to their daughter, Margaret M. Miller, in her work on the book and this she lovingly acknowledges. However, Ruth Miller personally spent days correcting and editing the manuscript; not once but several times.

We feel extraordinarily fortunate in having the cooperation of Dr. Marion Nelson, Director of the Norwegian-American Museum in Decorah, Iowa, and leading authority on Norwegian art and culture. Dr. Nelson corrected and helped revise the first two chapters and wrote the Preface.

Other friends who made personal contributions are: rosemaler Ethel Kvalheim who checked the chapter on "Color"; rosemaler Agnes Rykken of Seattle, Washington; Egil Larsen who helped with translation; and Rosalie and Bob Ekdale and Alice and Bill Lindquist for providing bed, board and fellowship to Sigmund on his travels while working on the book.

Lastly, to all our other rosemaling allies and good friends who are not mentioned by name but, who with unfailing interest stimulated us to push on, we say "mange tusen tak."

MARGARET M. MILLER and SIGMUND AARSETH

This chest is painted by Thomas Luraas, considered to be the grand master of rosemalers. A Telemark painter, Luraas' work is distinguished by being of a very high artistic and creative level. Copyright: © Photos Norge

PREFACE

ROSEMALING has had a unique relation to America for almost a hundred and fifty years. It was the last of the folk arts to develop in Norway and was therefore still at its height when mass immigration from that country began in the second quarter of the nineteenth century. It was also most highly developed in the inland valleys of Norway from where the great majority of early immigrants came. Since the possibilities of agricultural or other industrial expansion in these areas were too limited to absorb the increasing population, exodus was the only means of survival. Most of the painters were also cotters, or small landholders, the group that suffered most from population growth and therefore the one from which emigration was greatest. In his study of rosemaling in the province of Telemark, Oystein Vesaas makes reference to about twenty established painters who emigrated to America.

The favorite object for rosemaling decoration in Norway was the dowry, or storage, trunk. This piece of furniture became the standard luggage of the immigrant. As a consequence, examples of rosemaling came to America in even greater numbers than the painters who produced this art. Though none of these circumstances led to a rosemaling tradition's developing in the early pioneer settlements, rosemaling has been the folk art that has enjoyed the greatest revival among Norwegian-Americans since the 1930's.

The connections between rosemaling and America in the past have been largely due to historic circumstances. Now a more significant relationship is being established. The revival began in the immigrant group, but it soon attracted the attention of a broader American public. Rosemaling is now found in adult education programs, and arts-and-crafts schools in many areas where the Norwegian immigrant population is nominal. Arts and crafts such as crewel embroidery and overshot weaving, which came to America at the time of its early settlement, have long since become a part of American tradition and are not ordinarily associated with the group who introduced them. This is not generally true of the arts and crafts introduced by the later immigrants, though some of these, such as the egg dyeing of the Slavic peoples, are still extensively practiced within the immigrant communities. It appears that rosemaling may be among the first of these skills to be absorbed into the New World culture, and one cannot help but speculate on why it should enjoy this distinction.

For having originated as a folk art, rosemaling is an astonishingly sophisticated style of decorative painting. Firmly rooted in baroque and rococo traditions, and given its distinctive form by the people who seven centuries earlier carried the great animal style of northern Europe to its highest development in such monuments as the portals of the Urnes stave church, rosemaling is a free and flexible art that allows for considerable individual expression. It is a dynamic art in which "C" and "S" curves are combined to form either symmetrical or asymmetrical designs. These gain their unity from having one focal point in which all movement originates and from being painted in a rather limited number of consistently toned-down colors that are well balanced one against the other. The decoration acquires its expressive quality largely from the nature of the movements and counter-movements established by its ever curving lines. Unlike most folk painting, rosemaling also allows for the blending of colors to add richness and subtlety to its decorative and expressive character.

Because of its maturity as a style, rosemaling can relate rather directly to twentieth-century Americans and need not depend for its appeal on national or romantic associations. This undoubtedly accounts for the rapidity with which it is acquiring a place among the popular decorative arts of America. This also makes the kind of presentation which rosemaling is here given by Sigmund Aarseth and Margaret M. Miller long overdue.

December 14, 1972   MARION JOHN NELSON
                                       Professor of Art History
                                       University of Minnesota and
                                       Director, Norwegian-American Museum
                                       Decorah, Iowa

Contents

A mirror painted by Sigmund Aarseth in the "Binkhaven Nord" home of the Dean Maddens. A wood-graining treatment has been applied to the beams.
Copyright: © Photos Norge

NORWEGIAN ROSEMALING

The peace and serenity of a Norwegian farm. Copyright: © Photos Norge

WARM IS THE HEART OF NORWAY

Bright are the days in Norway
As June's flowers burst forth
From soil, warming to a sun
Too young to sleep.

Dark are the nights of Norway
When the moon struggles to break
Above the jagged mountains' peak,
And stars, sentinels standing at their stations,
Tell all; who will but look,
This Northland is ours!

Tall are the trees of Norway,
Spruce and pine and fir
Tough from winds
that flexed them strong,
With roots, grasping granite
As they search for soil
and sustenance.

Deep are the fjords of Norway
Knarled fingers of land
Clawing at the seas
As if land's last hope
Depended on their holding.

Still are the mists of Norway
Silence, broken only by man's intrusion
In ships, and buoys with bells
Bobbing on quiet waters.

Blue are the lakes of Norway
Clear as the sparkling streams
that feed and relieve them,
Spawning spots for trout
And salmon, and joy
In the hearts and minds of fishermen.

Wild are the falls of Norway
As snow, having months before
Lost its wings and fallen
in high places,
Uses summer, as a butterfly transformed
Finds new ways to move again.

Over cliffs and down valleys it spills,
  Gathering unto itself its own kind
    and power
  Until finally, with a roar in spring,
    Or a whisper in autumn,
  It finds its fjord, and peace.

Cold are the winds of Norway
  As summer, south retreating,
    Seeks the sun and milder places.

Warm is the heart of Norway
  Surrounding us with things we love
    Woven forever into the fabric
      of our family.

Painted with designs and colors unique
  Carved in panels and bowls and chests
    Baked in ovens and broiled in flame
      Poured into and out of tankards
  Pounded from iron on a fiery forge
    Into designs outliving our fathers
      and even our fathers' fathers.

A heritage, standing fair and tall
  With arms outstretching.
    Yes, *warm* is the heart of Norway!

Dean E. Madden
February 29, 1972

Figure 1. The prow of a Viking ship housed in the Norsk Folkemuseum at Bygdoy, Oslo, Norway. Copyright: © Photos Norge

1
The Roots of Rosemaling

NORWEGIAN ROSEMALING is a colorful and distinctive folk art unique to the small green valleys and high rugged mountains of Norway. Its mother, in a country where there are long, cold winter nights, was a deeply felt yearning for the warm and bright flowers that come to this Northland only with the summer sun. If this be so, its father was a centuries-old culture steeped in the love of ornamental forms of art.

Rosemaling was born as a definite style of interior decorative painting in the early 1700's and was nearly obsolete by the end of the 1800's. The reason it never completely died out is that a few craftsmen up in the valleys continued the old traditions and handed them down through their families.

To get a perspective on the development of rosepainting let us briefly examine some pertinent stages of Norwegian art history that led directly to it. It will then be apparent that though the rosemaling period of less than two hundred years was a relatively short one, it did not just appear but evolved naturally from an ancient cultural background.

About 800 A.D. the dynamic age of the Viking came thrusting out of history, to leave ample evidence of the feeling for beautiful lines and love of rich ornamentation that developed during this era. The major link to rosemaling from this period comes from remnants of metal work and, especially, wood-carving. Appearing time after time are the earliest Viking animal motifs, or "ribbon animals," so called because they were carved in a semi-abstract manner, with elongated interlacing loops reminiscent of ribbons. Slightly later, and representing the period of the Oseberg ship, came the old Nordic motif of the serpent struggling with animals. These writhing animals, known as the "gripping beasts" because of the way their mouths grip each other, are representative of a more complex interlacing that developed as the adventurous Vikings expanded their area of travel and came into contact with other cultures.

4

Figure 2. Detail of Viking
carving on the prow of the
Oseberg ship. Copyright:
© Photos Norge

Figure 3. Medieval carved
winged dragons. Copyright:
© Photos Norge

The acanthus leaf, one of the earliest rosemaling forms, developed as an art motif in Greece and Rome and was picked up by roving Vikings in the ninth century. It now took its place along with the earlier zoomorphic forms and can be seen springing out of the animals' extremities, most usually the mouth or tail. Finally, plant motifs alone became of major importance in the late Viking period. Rosemaling continues the characteristically complex curving and interlacing of the organic decorations of the Viking Age. These carvings are imbued not only with the strength and restless energy of their time, but testify to an art form far advanced for this period. If they suggest the baroque style, it is with every justification. The scrolls and foliage of the seventeenth-century Italian baroque, so popular in late rosemaling, give the same effect as this early Viking art carving.

An interesting aspect of the Viking period is that artistic endeavor was given great encouragement, despite the fact that, historically, Vikings are renowned for their warlike exploits. The great kings and chieftains gathered together the finest artists of their various principalities and encouraged their creativity. Artists were able to learn from each other and teach the young craftsmen under their tutelage, a much richer environment for creative work was generated, and it actually produced the rudimentary beginnings of the craft schools for which Norway is renowned.

During the waning years of the Viking Age came a final effort to carve animals in the earlier Viking tradition. Designated the "Urnes style," this carving takes the form of a simplified serpent design on the portals of the Urnes stave church; the latter is believed to date from the early 1100's, or the end of the Viking era. The figures on the portals— still in excellent condition—bear a remarkable resemblance to the "ribbon animals" which had heralded the beginnings of Viking art carving

Figure 5. Ancient Viking woodcarving in the form of "ribbon animals" on the oldest of the stave churches, Urnes, believed to have been built about 1100 A.D. or the end of the Viking era. Copyright: © Photos Norge

Figure 6. Borgund stave church. Notice the unique blend of Christian crosses with the pagan dragon's head. Copyright: © Photos Norge

about three hundred years previously. That these styles survive is due to the Norwegians' tenacious adherence to old traditions and is one of the reasons why rosepainting represents a continuing link with historic art forms.

During the Middle Ages Christianity was cemented throughout Norway, and its greatest contribution to historic art culture, the richly decorated stave church, was developed. Exceptional examples of the strength of tradition, these churches were mostly constructed in the twelfth and thirteenth centuries and were worthy successors to the great heritage of skill in wood-building that Norway had already demonstrated in the construction of Viking ships. One of the great evidences of this skill is that 1,300 to 1,600 stave churches are believed to have existed in Norway. Of these, only thirty remain, most having been destroyed or ruined by neglect. These remaining thirty are protected by the Norwegian government and bear testimony to the unique construction and superb workmanship that enabled them to withstand the damaging climate of Norway and survive to be the oldest wooden buildings in Europe.

The most prominent decorative art work of this age was the wood carving which appeared in the stave churches. This carving retained many of the Viking characteristics, with the acanthus leaf motif being enlarged upon. The acanthus now appeared not only on the serpent's anatomy as before, but began to be used to form its own separate designs. Stave churches became replete with intricately carved portals, capitals, arches, doors, pews, and lecterns.

The gloriously creative Middle Ages came to an end on a disastrous note. About 1349 the Black Death engulfed Norway, killing an estimated one-third to one-half of the entire population. Whole farms and valleys

Figure 7. Exterior of Garmo stave church now in the outdoor museum, Maihaugen, in Lillehammer, Norway. Copyright: De Sandvigske Samlinger

Figure 8. Interlacing carving on the north door portal of Lom stave church. Notice the use of the acanthus leaf in the woodcarving. Copyright: De Sandvigske Samlinger

Figure 9. Pulpit in Lom stave church. The baroque carving is ca. 1790 and is painted with traditional colors. The woodcarver was Jakob Sæterdalen. Copyright: De Sandvigske Samlinger

Figure 10. Interior of Lom stave church. Copyright: De Sandvigske Samlinger

Figure 11. Closeup of the combination of baroque acanthus carving and Renaissance painting in the chancel of Lom stave church. Copyright: De Sandvigske Samlinger

Figure 12. The beautifully carved and painted pulpit in Øye church. The trees are typical of Valdres area rosemaling. Copyright: © Photos Norge

were completely depopulated, and with the ensuing struggle for survival and lack of manpower most of the stave churches fell into decay and were eventually torn down. It was not until the late Renaissance period of the 1600's and 1700's that artists began to redecorate the churches. For the first time wall paintings began to appear in the remaining stave churches; these gradually led to the lavish ornamental painting on the vaults, walls, and lectern canopies so admired today. This painting was mostly done by town artists who came into the valleys and, together with wood carving, it became a forerunner of the rosemaling soon to come.

During the 1600's the baroque style which was then popular in most of Europe reached Norway. This strong, straight type of ornamentation was adapted to Norwegian church decoration until it, in turn, was eclipsed in popularity, in the 1700's, by a new style. This ornate art form, called rococo, was based on the highly decorated curved line; while used somewhat in church decoration, it became more popular as a style for rosemaling in the homes. Both baroque and rococo decorative styles became adapted to the Norwegian temperament and were used with more informality and greater vividness than elsewhere in Europe. Rarely was any

Figure 13. The altar in Øye church. Copyright: © Photos Norge

Figure 14. Decorative painting from the chancel in Lom stave church. Paintings depicting the life of Christ were common in early church painting. Copyright: De Sandvigske Samlinger

Figure 15. Decorative renaissance painting in Tretten church showing the influence of baroque. Copyright: De Sandvigske Samlinger

one style used exclusively at any one time in the churches. From the medieval to the rococo, many styles were blended into a unique and fascinating whole.

Norwegian craftsmanship was not limited to Viking ships and stave churches. The same skills, materials, and technical principles were used to construct the farm buildings which were about to receive rosepainting.

A Norwegian farm house was a place of work, but it also meant warm and wonderful things to the family who lived in it. It was a peaceful, cozy place to spend the cold, dark winter months, and a haven from the elements. It was an assembly place and a center for social occasions.

Figure 16. Interior of Uvdal stave church. The wall painting on the left shows a marked Dutch influence while baroque and rococo decoration have also been used. Copyright: © Photos Norge

It was also a source of great pride to its owner, but unknown to him, at least by southern European standards of the sixteenth century, it was quite primitive, dark, and sooty.

These early homes had only small or no glass windows. In fact, a glass window only a few inches square was at that time of such great value that its owner was considered well-to-do. If he moved, he took his glass window along.

An open hearth in the center of a main room was used to cook and provide heat. An opening in the roof above the hearth let out the smoke. The transparent membrane of a cow's stomach, stretched over a frame, served to close the opening while still allowing a little light to penetrate the darkness. It was drab and gloomy.

In order to brighten up the home for festive occasions, brightly colored woven tapestries were hung along the timbered walls. After the celebration, however, they were quickly taken down so they would not be darkened by soot.

It was not until the latter part of the sixteenth century that the idea of a contained fireplace and chimney finally reached the Norwegian

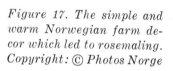

Figure 17. The simple and warm Norwegian farm decor which led to rosemaling. Copyright: © Photos Norge

valleys, and two hundred years were to pass before they became customary in the farm house. Corner fireplaces made of local soft soapstone and sometimes decorated with carving then became popular throughout Scandinavia. Once the smoke could go up the chimney, flue dirt and soot became controllable. Clean air and cheaper glass made light more plentiful. Eventually it became common practice to clean up rooms that had been dirtied, in some cases, with hundreds of years of smoke by painting ceilings, walls, and woodwork, thus laying base coats for the colorful decoration to follow. This, together with improved economic conditions in Norway and the inspiring example of painted decoration in the local stave churches, laid the groundwork for rosemaling in the home.

Figure 19. This chest is a good example of early painting (Renaissance) and is a forerunner of what is actually considered to be "rosemaling." The similarity between this chest and church painting is quite obvious. Copyright: Norsk Folkemuseum (Oslo)

Other historical developments, seemingly unrelated, had definite influences on the development of this peasant art. New prosperity resulted not only from the relaxation of Danish rule, under which Norway had been since the late fourteenth century, but also from the breaking up of the old German Hanseatic League. Merchants of this league had, ever since 1294, held exclusive rights to carry on trade from Bergen and other important Norwegian ports. Norway traditionally has done well when using her own coastline, and this charter prevented the Norwegians themselves from benefiting from use of the sea. Now, newly-made overseas contacts not only began to improve Norway's standard of living, but also to broaden her provincial view of various forms of culture. Lumber exporting became a major industry. This was important in the development of rosemaling because it meant that inland farmers could sell their own lumber and thus reap the profits from resources they had previously been unable to exploit. New buildings and the modernization of old buildings resulted, calling for new types of interior treatment.

Another important influence on rosemaling at this time was the life-style of the farmer himself. Only by understanding this can we see why he developed and cultivated his folk art.

In Norway the farmer is called *bonde*. This term means "farmer" or "peasant" but signifies more than "just a farmer"—it denotes a very special status, that of freeholder. Unlike southern European countries during the Middle Ages, where most of the land was owned by a few wealthy landowners and worked by serfs, Norway had free farmers who owned their own land. This gave the farmer a spirit of independence almost totally unknown in European areas outside of Scandinavia and made possible the rise of a rural art. Under the feudal system, the serf had little time or money for artistic development.

Perhaps even more important, however, the *bonde* had a sense of possession of his land which in turn created a pride in his home, stimulating his desire to improve and beautify it. If a Norwegian farmer had a room decorated, he was assured it would continue to be in his family's estate for generations and he would be remembered by his family for it. He not infrequently had his name recorded by the artist as part of the decoration.

This assurance of possession came from special laws, unique to Scandinavia, which not even the king could override. The Odels Law, which simply states that a farm must be handed down from the father to the eldest son, or, lacking sons, to the eldest daughter, still exists. Also, a family is entitled to buy back its land from anyone outside the family at the original sale price for a certain number of years after the original date of sale. This law serves as a deterrent to outsiders' buying family land.

Thus the Norwegian *bonde* has always felt independent, regardless of the size of his farm. In a limited respect, he was a little "king" on his own land, a term which was sometimes used in referring to influential farmers. While the farms themselves were mostly small (only 3% of the land of Norway is tillable), a family often owned many acres of surrounding mountain land frequently as valuable as the farm land itself, not only for raising goats and cattle, but also for the hunting, timber, and fishing rights that went with it.

The Norwegian farmer's desire to express himself with his own art form was undoubtedly accelerated by the increased prosperity of the eighteenth century. Not infrequently the human tendency toward competition also crept into the picture as neighbor vied with neighbor to see who could have the most beautifully decorated rooms. Prestige has often been an element in art acquisition.

Decorative painting in homes began in the seacoast towns in Norway. Gradually the professional "town" painters branched out into the lowland areas to decorate churches and wealthier homes. Since the expense of hiring these professional painters to decorate farm rooms was usually beyond the purse of most *bønder*, and since transportation between the valleys was still quite difficult by 1700, farmers usually hired local artists who had demonstrated talent to work for them—sometimes providing only food and lodging as payment. Small messages left by the itinerant artists as inscriptions in their decorations give us delightful insights into some of their working problems and feelings. Several commentaries on the quantity of food served hungry artists were lettered among the scrolls. "The reason the roses are small here is because the potatoes are small," and, "This family was the salt of the earth, but they set a meager table" serve as humorous reminders of the scanty reward some of these early rosemalers received for their work.

Gradually rosemaling spread outward from the lowlands until it reached the highlands, or mountain districts. There it was fervently picked up by the people and adapted to their native style of decoration, a style closer to rosemaling as we think of it today than to mere popular decorative painting. Rosemaling flourished longer in these areas than in other sections of Norway and also developed a freer and fresher style than elsewhere in the country.

In spite of what has been said, the development of rosemaling does not appear to be related only to economic well-being. The Telemark and Hallingdal valleys were among the poorest farm areas, but they produced some of the greatest examples of rosemaling. It was not uncommon in these valleys to have two or even three famous district artists carry out decorations in one room. Even the poorer coastal districts of western Norway had their painters, though the challenge of sailing and fishing took great amounts of the time and energy of the young men growing up there. Most of the painting done in these districts was by amateur artists, for they obviously did not have time to evolve a high technical competency. Their work, however, was very individual, quaint, and charming.

Rosemaling is often thought to have developed because the farmers needed something to do in the long, dark winter nights. This undoubtedly had some influence on the profusion of artistic activity in the rural

Figure 20. Small chest decorated in a way common on the west coast of Norway, especially around Bergen where this painting was sometimes called "strilemaling" or "coast painting." Background was usually rust red with vivid colors. Copyright: Norsk Folkemuseum (Oslo)

areas of Norway, but it probably meant little more for rosemaling than for the other folk arts.

The development of a divergence in styles of rosepainting between various districts of Norway could have been caused by the differences between the people in the various valleys. It often seems that the characteristics of people are expressed through their various folk arts, such as music and embroidery, metal and woodwork, and rosemaling. This is especially true for a country such as Norway where the mountains isolate areas from each other. In the two predominant rosemaling districts of Hallingdal and Telemark, these differences are quite clear cut. The natives of the Hallingdal district like music which is highly rhythmical, strong, and dramatic. Their music has a distinct beat, their buildings are strong and sturdily built, and their embroidery is simple and dramatic. Hallingdal rosemaling is imbued with all these folk characteristics and is typically simple, well balanced, and strong. By contrast, the music of Telemark is lyrical, the lofts are intricate and well proportioned with elaborate woodwork, and the metalwork is complex and finely wrought down to the last detail. Telemark rosemaling followed these distinctions in craftsmanship and became lyrical and fine with exquisite details and intricate patterns. In spite of these district differences, there can be seen similarities in rosemaling designs which link the provinces together. These likenesses have endowed the total art of rosemaling with a flavor truly Norwegian.

When studying old rosemaling today, we realize the early masters were highly skilled craftsmen. A brief look at how this came to pass is in order. Frequently those with an artistic bent started training as apprentices while boys, preparing paints and doing other menial tasks

Figure 23. This bed, painted by the Telemark artist Ola Hansson, is notable for the strong use of the baroque tendril for which Hansson is famous. Copyright: Norsk Folkemuseum (Oslo)

for the masters. In this way they studied "basics," while picking up styles and techniques from the older experienced painters. This is perhaps another of the reasons why each valley developed its own distinct rosemaling style. Budding young rosepainters could not help absorbing some of their masters' style and techniques. To these the young painters adapted their own individual characteristics, adding to the further development of the art. Sometimes a talented young farmer was able to pick up enough from watching a visiting rosepainter to be able to start on his own, but this was the exception rather than the rule. Many old masters were quite jealous of their techniques and refused to share their hard-won knowledge with anyone, taking their secrets to the grave. Families in many Norwegian valleys carefully passed their rosemaling traditions down from generation to generation, a custom active to the present day. In Telemark, the Luraas and Hovde families, and in Hallingdal, the Sata family, are famous for an unbroken line of fine rosemalers.

Some of the rosemaling that contains figures is uniquely charming and primitive in quality. The figures are often painted on black backgrounds with a lack of perspective. This gives them a peculiarly innocent quality. Popular subjects for painting were the common folk of the day, biblical characters, popular heroes, and military men. The latter were usually depicted mounted on the little, stubby, blond horses of the Fjord districts. In this type of decoration, the figures were usually surrounded by flower motifs. They presented an extremely upright and dignified appearance while being decidedly quaint. Occasionally local trees were used as the focal points in designs. Pine trees, which grow thickly in Valdres and Østerdalen were frequently painted into the designs of those districts. Strangely, these trees often showed an almost Chinese influence in their style, particularly in Valdres.

As the population of Norway increased during the 1800's many good painters emigrated to America. This emigration was further encouraged by the passage of the American Homstead Act of 1862, which granted free land to people willing to settle on it. Norwegian tenant farmers and younger sons who would never inherit the family property were especially drawn to America. Gradually the Norwegians came inland, and

Figure 24. Early bowl from Telemark. Painted in 1798 by Seljord. Copyright: Norsk Folkemuseum (Oslo)

Figure 25. Two rosemaling masters from the famous Hallingdal rosemaling family called Sata. They are Nils Ellingsgard on the left and his cousin Lars Sata- øyen who painted the break- front they are standing in front of. Copyright: © Photos Norge

eventually they settled in the Midwest, largely in Wisconsin, Illinois, Iowa, and Minnesota. These four states now form an important nucleus of rosepainting activity in America. Making the land productive was the immigrant's first concern. As a result, little rosemaling was done in America until Per Lysne began rosepainting for a living in Stoughton, Wisconsin, during the 1930's.

Figure 29. Cupboard door from Fagernes Folkmuseum. Valdres style rosemaling. Copyright: © Photos Norge

Much credit for the revival of rosemaling that has taken place during the past decade in the United States must be given the Norwegian-American Museum in Decorah, Iowa. This museum, which houses Norwegian pioneer artifacts, has for the past five years, in cooperation with the Decorah community, sponsored an annual cultural festival called the

Figure 30. Chest from Fjot-
land with typical Vest-
Agder style rosemaling.
Copyright: Norsk Folke-
museum (Oslo)

Figure 31. Chest painted in
1853 from Eiken, Vest-
Agder. It is an unusual
combination of painting and
simple carving. Copyright:
Norsk Folkemuseum (Oslo)

Figure 32. Box from Vest-
Agder painted in 1862. The
straight lines and round
flowers are typical of this
district. Copyright: Norsk
Folkemuseum (Oslo)

Figure 33. Old rosemaled and carved sleigh from the museum at Fagernes, Norway. Copyright: © Photos Norge

Figure 34. Chest painted with the artist's own personal style but showing the influence of rococo. Copyright: Norsk Folkemuseum (Oslo)

Nordic Fest. In connection with this festival, it has held a nationally juried exhibition of rosemaling, a step that has been instrumental in revitalizing the art. It has brought leading rosemalers from Norway to teach classes and has organized several rosemaling tours to Norway. The museum also sends out a newsletter which keeps rosepainters up to date on the latest activities in the field, serves as a distributing point for publications on Nordic art and culture, and supplies some hard-to-find brushes and unpainted woodenware for rosemalers to decorate.

In Norway, rosemaling began to lose its freedom and freshness around 1850. The rococo style had so influenced Norway's folk art that it could no longer claim to be primitive, and its natural evolution had nowhere to go. There were several other factors that also may have helped precipitate this gradual stagnation. One was the lack of interest in the

Figure 37. Chest painted in rococo style by Kristian Listad. This chest has great dynamic feeling and vividness. It is from Gudbrandsdal. Copyright: Norsk Folkemuseum (Oslo)

Figure 38. A small hanging cupboard from Lom, Oppland. Notice the similarity between the gracefully flowing rosemaling and the carving. Copyright: Norsk Folkemuseum (Oslo)

old folk culture among the more sophisticated city dwellers. This attitude permeated the rural districts of Norway, and some farmers came to believe the traditions of the old Norwegians did not have the value they had once given them. At approximately this same time the Industrial Revolution, which changed life-styles in the country and the cities, was on the upswing. People became more interested in producing and purchasing mass-produced items. Handcrafted work was no longer as sought after as it had once been, and so it began to fade out. Fortunately this attitude no longer prevails. The rebirth of interest in handcrafts has been largely due to the efforts of societies and schools that have made the preservation of the home crafts and individual arts their mission.

During the first half of the twentieth century in Norway, little serious interest was shown in the rural arts by the general public. A letter sent to Oslo in 1950 inquiring about possibilities for taking lessons in rosemaling was answered by the statement, "Rosemaling is a dead art." In recent years, however, the younger generation of city folk have experienced a revival of interest in their cultural heritage and are now beginning to take pride in the life and art of their countryside. They have gone into the mountains and have discovered, in the remnants of their old culture, a charm and beauty they were unable to appreciate before. Conversely, with easy and economical means of transportation, the rural youth are coming to the towns for education and bringing their heritage of folk arts and customs with them. Thus the wonderful freshness of rosemaling is reviving in its native land and once more the love of rich traditional colors and designs is developing to offset the impersonal and austere feeling that mass-produced articles can give contemporary homes.

Figure 39. The charming elderly gentleman pictured here is Norway's most illustrious rosemaler, Herr Knut K. Hovden. Descendant of the renowned Telemark rosemaling family called "Hovde," he deserves great credit for keeping rosemaling alive during this century. Not only did Herr Hovden teach at the craft school in Sand, Norway, for thirty-two years, but he spent his summers traveling through southern Norway to find, study, and reproduce the most valuable of the older, high quality rosemaling. Born in 1893, this remarkable man still paints every day at his home next to the Sand Yrkesskule. Copyright: Margaret M. Miller

2
Hidden Norway

To DEVELOP A FEELING for how rosemaling was originally used in homes, picture rustic farm buildings nestled in valleys and among the lower mountain slopes, surrounded by neatly tilled fields and orchards. Due to the rough mountain terrain, farms were often far apart, forming little worlds of their own. This was particularly true in the case of larger farms, which sometimes included thirty or forty wooden buildings.

The buildings on a farm were usually small, and each had its specialized function. A *stue* (which means dwelling) was used for living purposes. The one-story *veslebur* and the two-story *stabbur* were used as storehouses for food supplies and equipment. There were cattle and goat sheds, and it was quite common to have a sauna type bath house featuring a stone oven which, when heated and splashed with water, produced an exhilarating and relaxing steam bath. On some of the more prosperous farms, a quaint tower contained a bell that was rung to summon workers from the fields for meals.

Nearly all inland Norwegian farm buildings were of log construction, a natural building material in Norway where huge areas are still covered with virgin forests. Much of their building style is pre-Viking and, according to tradition, was brought to Norway from Russia. Log construction was admirably suited to the rigorous weather conditions in both countries since thick logs provided good insulating qualities. When caulked with moss and coated with a tar pitch, the logs sealed buildings tightly.

Fir and pine were the most common material for log construction. After topping, the tree was often allowed to stand in place for several years, exposed to the elements, drying slowly to reduce checking. This weathering and drying process, plus the many coats of tar that were applied after the building was constructed, partly explain why these buildings have endured, in many cases, for up to eight hundred years.

32

Figure 40. Entrance to a farm complex in the outdoor museum, Maihaugen (De Sandvigske Samlinger), at Lillehammer, Norway. Copyright: © Photos Norge

Figure 41. Øygarden, a typical "cluster" farm from Skjåk, so called because of the random clustering of the buildings around several courtyards. Copyright: De Sandvigske Samlinger

Figure 42. Early log con-
struction of buildings with
a bell tower. Copyright: De
Sandvigske Samlinger

Figure 43. Early log house
with enclosed porch from
Skjåk. Copyright: De Sandvigske Samlinger

The roofs of some buildings were covered with several overlaying layers of birch bark upon which sod was placed in double layers. The first layer of sod was laid green-side-down, thus providing a soil base upon which the second layer was placed, green-side-up. These growing turf roofs have become a hallmark of old Norwegian farm buildings and remain a distinguishing feature to this day. Grass, flowers, and even small trees grow profusely on these roofs, providing coolness from the summer sun and warmth from the winter's cold.

The simple and austere appearance that log construction gives Norwegian farm buildings disguised the decorated interior of the living area and is the reason we have titled this chapter "Hidden Norway." How many hundreds of tourists have taken the classic tours of Norway from Oslo to Bergen and passed by these lovely old buildings, never dreaming of the hidden beauty in painted decorations just inside their doors!

One of the most unique and picturesque buildings in the Norwegian farm grouping is the two-story *stabbur*, or "loft." The lower floor most often was used for the storage of smoked meat, fish, and grain. The second floor was used for storage of more valuable family possessions (thus the profusion of gaily painted trunks) or as a guest room. Often, an enclosed cantilevered gallery was constructed around the second floor, giving the loft its chalet appearance. Supporting foundations for lofts were mounted on stone pillars that held the building off the ground for several feet. The room comprising the second story of the *stue* (dwelling) was occasionally decorated with rosemaling. A farmer could indicate his wealth by the size of his loft and the abundance of decoration in the guest room.

Figure 44. Typical sod roofs at Hjellarstua in Skjåk. Copyright: De Sandvigske Samlinger

The outside of most older farm buildings in the interior of the country were not painted. Exteriors were sometimes richly carved, and this carving, interspersed with fancy profiles sawed from flat boards, made the construction of portals, galleries, and stairways more interesting.

During the 1800's, some buildings were treated with pine tar that with age brought out lovely details in the construction and carving. Tar acted not only as a preservative, but it highlighted areas of the buildings since it turned yellow where the sun struck it and remained dark in the shadows. Thus the patina of age created a rich but subdued effect.

An interesting characteristic of early Norwegian buildings is the entrance door, built low and wide. A building was usually entered from an open or enclosed porch (*sval*). Two doors and the *sval* served to protect the entrance from buffeting winds and blowing snow. The low entrance also made it necessary to enter the house bent over, giving the owner of the home an advantage if the person coming in was unfriendly.

If a home had a second floor, an outside unheated stairway led up from the *sval*. Lofts also had an outside stairway to the second floor, but sometimes there was merely a ladder from the front *sval* up to the gallery, which was pulled up for safety's sake once the people entered the second story.

Roof construction of buildings varied from area to area, but in many of the inland districts a popular construction was rafters resting on large

Figure 45. The exterior of a loft at Longvik farm in Rauland, Telemark, which has been intricately decorated with carving. Copyright: © Photos Norge

Figure 46. Low door at a farm loft in Skjåk. Note support posts for cantilevered second story. Copyright: De Sandvigske Samlinger

Figure 47. Interior of an old farm home in the collection of buildings in the outdoor museum called Maihaugen (De Sandvigske Samlinger) at Lillehammer, Norway. Copyright: Photos Norge

beams running from gable to gable. This made ceiling panels admirably suited to rosemaling, since either the space between the beams, the beams themselves, or both could be richly decorated.

The interior construction of early Norwegian farm houses did not change radically for centuries. Massive beams and the simplicity of the log construction gave rooms an architectural strength which later provided a perfect contrast to the graceful flowers and tendrils of rosemaling.

With the advent of fireplaces and chimneys, a second story could be added or a partial loft placed over the downstairs chamber. The loss of the smoke hole made windows necessary, and with windows came a new lightness and airiness. At about the same time earth floors were replaced by wood, and finally, major pieces of early Norwegian furniture began to be built against the walls of the room and often were joined together. This gave even a small room the largest possible area of free floor space. With the development of the light and open interior came an interest in decorating furniture.

Expanded foreign trade led to the influence of Renaissance cabinet-work from central and southern Europe. Furniture from Holland was imported into most urban and some rural areas of Norway. Its beautifully designed paneling, edged with fine moldings, gave Nowegian carpenters the impetus they needed to develop a type of furniture which later was decorated with rosemaling. Thus the carpenter craftsmen, often unknowingly, played as great a part as the rosepainters themselves in creating the fine Norwegian decorative furniture we know today. Interestingly, in many cases, the carpenter and painter were the same man.

A typical room in an old Norwegian farm dwelling had benches built along the wall, with a long table in front and a free-standing bench on the other side of the table. The "high seat," reserved from Viking times as the special place for the head of the house, was always situated at the end of the long board (table), in the corner near a window. In olden days the high seat was the most important thing in the home and was brought with a family whenever they moved. Here the husband would sit to make family decisions or perhaps read the Bible while his children sat around the long board. It is told that on one of the Viking expeditions, the sailors tossed their high seat posts into the sea as they approached land. As the posts were carried by the waves and currents, the Viking ships followed them. Where the posts were washed ashore was the spot the superstitious Vikings, following an old tradition, chose to settle, and there they founded the city known as Reykjavik.

There was usually a built-in bunk near the fireplace for the farmer and his wife. The children slept in a side room or in a low loft above it. Beds were short and wide, so the occupants slept in a half-sitting or curled position. There was usually a wooden canopy overhead and a storage area or pullout bed below. A great deal of the finest rosemaling was devoted to decorating such beds. Adjoining the beds were cabinets and a hutch or two, and many homes had a treasured grandfather's clock, also decorated with rosemaling, that reached from floor to ceiling. The fireplace in the corner was the gathering place of the family and servants during the long evenings.

Figure 48. An example of "kroting" or chalk painting, the earliest form of decoration in Norwegian farm homes. This type of ornamentation was usually rendered for the holidays. Copyright: © Photos Norge

The first type of painted decoration in Norwegian homes you find on the West Coast and has a direct connection with Viking times. On festival occasions, the walls of these early homes were covered with tapestries that hung from a wide border around the wall beneath the ceiling. This border was originally covered with a woven band called a "refill." The tapestries and refill were both known to have been used in Viking halls, and fragments of refills were found in the Oseberg ship. Later the refill was replaced with decorative chalk painting or "kroting," usually applied in a simple, geometric style directly to the dark walls with white chalk. Sometimes the design was drawn in black and red on a white background. The kroting border was women's work in those days and was regularly repainted for holidays. There are homes on the West Coast where the kroting is still intact on the upper parts of the walls. One was seen recently where the kroting had been redone by the old grandmother who, continuing in the footsteps of her ancestors, made use of a decorative skill that represents the living end of a painting tradition lasting nearly a thousand years.

Rosemaling was often first introduced into the rural homes on smaller objects such as ale bowls, tankards, and chests, which gave color to the simple farm interior. The idea of painting such household equipment may have originated with the professional painters who came from the cities to work on the churches. Sometimes these men decorated ale bowls and tankards in their spare time and the peasants probably felt such decorations enhanced their own rustic living conditions.

The most important inspiration for decorating major areas of farm homes came from the churches. Here an abundance of paintings suggested the graceful scrolls and flowers originally painted with chalk on ceilings in the farm homes. From there rosemaling began to cover walls, beds, doors, and furniture. Surprisingly, instead of producing the overdecorated effect one would expect from such profuse ornamentation, the rooms developed an atmosphere of gaiety that was rustic and charming.

Figure 49. Simple plate showing the type of rosemaling first introduced into homes. Copyright: De Sandvigske Samlinger

Figure 50. Box from the Sauherad area of Telemark with early, primitive rosemaling. Copyright: Norsk Folkemuseum (Oslo)

The most popular piece of furniture decorated was the dowry chest. Eligible Norwegian girls often had such a chest to keep the treasures they were making to start their own homes. Even if a family was poor and could afford no other painting, they managed to decorate a dowry chest. Many of these chests have been preserved in museums, with colors as fresh and rich as the day they were painted. Usually the decoration included the marriage year. The bride's initials or name as well as that of her father were also added. Many chests were painted by untutored farmers who could not afford to pay a professional artist, so the decorations were simple and primitive. On the other hand, when they could afford them, highly skilled rosepainters covered the chests lavishly with intricate scrolls and blooms so that scarcely an inch of background area was left undecorated. Sometimes the inside lid of the dowry chest was decorated with chalk painting, but the outside was always done with oils.

Most furniture dating from the 1700's and later, the so called "golden age" of rosepainting, had beautifully designed paneling surrounded by handsome molding. Major panels were often deeply recessed and painted a contrasting color from that of the smaller surrounding panels. The largest panels received the most important design. If the design was geometric, the smaller designs, by contrast, were sometimes flowing scrollwork, or vice versa. The upper portions of the furniture (near the ceiling) were frequently topped by heavy and ornately designed cornices. If the ceiling was high, a strongly decorative molding was also added where the walls joined the ceiling. These moldings were often decorated with "lasur" glazing (a transparent film of color used to cover furniture

Figure 51. Beautifully decorated dowry chest from Hallingdal. Crosshatching has been intricately and skillfully used in the painting. Copyright: De Sandvigske Samlinger

Figure 52. Early rosemaling on a bed at Longvik farm and tourist inn in Telemark. Copyright: Photos Norge

and walls), and complemented the more decorative panels. Beams were frequently painted to match a design used predominantly on several other pieces of furniture, such as beds. Some beams were decorated with rosemaling on the sides and a geometric pattern on the bottom. Ceilings between beams could also be decorated, and sometimes the painting extended over the beams as well as the ceilings. This was often true in the painting of the famous Telemark artist, Ola Hansson, who covered entire rooms, including log walls, ceilings, beams, beds, doors, door panels and cupboards, leaving little area in a room undecorated. In some rooms walls would be stippled with lasur, while the beams and various pieces of furniture were rosepainted. The variety was endless, yet consistent within a tradition and extremely disciplined and lovely.

It is of great interest and utmost importance to consider the colors that the rosemalers favored because they are unique to Norway and give rosemaling so much of its distinctive flavor. This will be done in detail in Chapter 4.

Figure 53. Cupboard door painted with typical Telemark fine line work. Copyright: Photos Norge

3
Materials and Preparation for Painting

MATERIALS AND SUPPLIES FOR ROSEMALING

CERTAIN BASIC EQUIPMENT is needed by all beginning rosemalers. These supplies are listed below with no unnecessary items included. A supplementary list of equipment for advanced students and teachers follows later in the chapter.

BASIC SUPPLIES

> A box to hold supplies—a shoe box will do to begin with
> Old rags
> A ruler
> Pencils (soft lead type), chalk and charcoal
> A jar of white vaseline
> 2 jars or 2 can tops—jars are best, about baby-food size
>   —can tops of the type found on shaving cream cans
> An apron or smock
> A roll of tape—scotch or masking
> A palette knife
> A palette—either a disposable paper tear-off palette
>   (large size 12″ x 16″) or a suitable pan such as a pizza pan
> A pad of tracing paper
> A bottle of turpentine or odorless thinner
> A bottle or can of boiled, unbleached linseed oil
> Several sheets of fine sand paper
> Some newspaper for protecting surrounding areas
> Panels of masonite board, ¼″ or ⅜″ thick—untempered—
>   approximately 14″ x 18″ size

All these supplies can be found either in the home or at an art supply store except for the masonite (pressed wood) board which can be purchased from your local lumber yard. The yard will usually want you to buy the masonite as they get it, in a 4′ x 8′ sheet. If you want to have the entire sheet of masonite cut up to your specifications, most lumber yards will charge a small fee, but it is well worth the time it saves. Sometimes you will be able to buy scrap pieces of masonite that will be large enough for practicing on at a saving, so it is wise to ask at the yard if they have any scraps on hand.

The use of most of these supplies is fairly evident. The vaseline is used to lubricate the brushes between painting sessions, and the small jars or caps are used to hold linseed oil and turpentine. If you pour some linseed oil into the cap of the jar holding the oil it makes a convenient container for dipping your brushes into during the painting and is shallow enough to allow you to see how much oil you are getting on your brush each time. The pencil, chalk, and charcoal are used for sketching or tracing designs. Carbon paper is not recommended, as it leaves a waxy residue that will resist the paint and keep it from adhering to the surface. If you feel strongly that you want to use carbon paper, ask for graphite paper. Masonite is the best surface upon which to do your first rosemaling, as it allows you to practice on a fairly large area that has the feeling of a wood surface and yet is easily handled. It can be turned, held on the lap, or placed on a table. All masonite boards must be painted with a semi-gloss paint before you can begin rosemaling.

Thinners

Linseed oil is an oil pressed from the seeds of the flax plant. *Boiled linseed oil* is a further refinement of linseed oil, and it is the preferred substance for mixing with oil paints. This oil ranges in color from light amber to a pale golden color, depending on the amount of bleaching the oil has been given during the processing. A darker color is usually pre-

Figure 54. Dipping the brush in oil in a bottle top. Copyright: Margaret M. Miller

ferred by rosemalers, as the paler oil has a tendency to darken with age and could change the color of the paint slightly. It has even been known to change the background. This is the reason most authorities recommend that you buy the unbleached linseed oil. If you are using oil that has been standing around the house for some time check its age and usability as indicated by its clarity.

Stand oil, a favorite of some rosemalers, is raw linseed oil that has been heated and allowed to stand at a temperature of 525–575° for a time. As a result, it undergoes certain chemical changes. It is heavy or thick, similar to honey, and must be thinned with turpentine to a suitable painting consistency. Some rosemalers prefer stand oil chiefly because it imparts a leveling quality to paints with which it is mixed. This means that the paint dries remarkably free from brush marks and has a smoother, more enamel-like look. Unfortunately, this shiny, brilliant appearance is just the opposite of the natural, fresh look that most rosemalers have always sought to achieve. The printed appearance of a design painted with stand oil can be likened more to china painting than to rosemaling and, additionally, an overuse of stand oil can cause paint to crack.

Turpentine, the distilled sap of pine trees, is the preferred thinner of most oil painters. It comes in one grade only, "pure gum spirits of turpentine," and that is all the purchaser need look for when buying it. Turpentine is the most commonly used thinner because of its pleasing odor and low fire risk due to rapid evaporation, and yet it allows sufficient time for the painting operation. Until recently turpentine was used almost exclusively by professional rosemalers, but now various paint thinners have come on the market which are designated "odorless." These thinners are less expensive than turpentine and do an adequate job, while helping to eliminate the headaches and tired feeling that some painters get from smelling turpentine over a period of several hours. Whether you use turpentine or another thinner be sure to keep the container closed when it is not in use.

Paints

Ivory Black	Venetian Rèd
Titanium White	Burnt Umber
(Titanium-Zinc White is best if you can find it)	Raw Umber
	Chromium Oxide Green
Burnt Sienna	Viridian
Raw Sienna	Cobalt Blue
Yellow Ochre–light	Prussian Blue
Cadmium Red–light	

Paints with trade names such as Rembrandt, Winsor-Newton, Grumbacher, Weber, London Oil, and Shiva are all reliable in quality. Rembrandt, a Dutch product, is the finest oil paint obtainable, while Winsor-

Newton, a British product, is a close second. Rembrandt may be difficult to find in the United States, as it is not as widely distributed as some of the other brands. Grumbacher is the leading American oil paint and is excellent but not quite as finely ground or as pure in hue as Rembrandt or Winsor-Newton. Since it is the most distributed brand in the United States it is probably the one you will find most readily, especially if you live in a small town. Shiva, a Grumbacher product, and London Oil, a Winsor-Newton product, are economy quality paints for students and are fine for the beginning rosemaler.

It is a wise idea to purchase the larger tubes (1.25 fl. oz.) of white, yellow ochre, and burnt umber. These colors are generally used in greatest quantity and are less costly in the long run when bought in the economy size than the small ⅜ fl. oz. tubes. The best white is a combination of titanium- and zinc-white, which contains the admirable qualities of both whites. However, most rosemalers use just titanium, as the titanium-zinc white combination is rather hard to find. Permanent Pigment oil colors, a Taubes product, makes titanium-zinc white, but this is a brand not commonly carried by art stores.

Brushes

In order to do rosemaling, several types of brushes are required. Each part of a design beginning with the large scroll strokes and continuing down to the final outlining strokes requires its special brush of a particular shape and size. Since Telemark and Hallingdal are the most popular styles of rosemaling, the brushes for both of these techniques will be recommended.

In Telemark style the brushes are both flat and round, the flat ones being used to paint the basic strokes and the round ones doing the outlining. Hallingdal uses only round brushes for both basic and outlining strokes.

The following listings are, firstly, of the number and type of brushes needed for each style and, secondly, of the companies that manufacture good quality brushes and the series numbers by which these brushes may be ordered. Most art supply stores stock the flat brushes in one brand or another, but it is uncommon to find the large round Hallingdal brushes and the outlining brushes in regular stock. You will probably have to have the store order them from a catalogue, unless the store handles brushes especially for rosemalers. The Norwegian-American Museum is one of the best sources for rosemaling brushes and is prompt to fill any orders it receives.

Brushes for Telemark style painting:
    Flat red sable—1 each of sizes 10, 8, 6
    Round red sable—1 each of sizes 3, 2
Brushes for Hallingdal style painting:
    Round red sable—1 each of sizes 10, 8, 5, 3

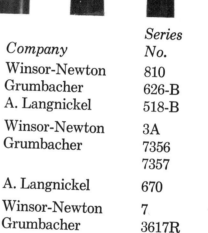

Hallingdal, basic and outlining

*Figure 55.
Telemark, basic*

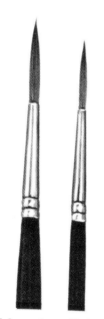

Telemark, outlining

Style	Company	Series No.	Recommended Sizes
Telemark, basic	Winsor-Newton	810	10, 8, 6
	Grumbacher	626-B	same
	A. Langnickel	518-B	same
Telemark, outlining	Winsor-Newton	3A	3, 2
	Grumbacher	7356	same
		7357	(extra long)
	A. Langnickel	670	same
Hallingdal, basic and outlining	Winsor-Newton	7	10, 8, 5, 3
	Grumbacher	3617R	20, 16, 10, 6

Winsor-Newton makes superior brushes, and Langnickel and Grumbacher are of good quality, too. But regardless of the manufacturer, when selecting brushes do *not* settle for brushes of lesser quality than red sable. It is essential that the hairs of *all* brushes, whether flat or round, cling together, and that each brush keep its shape through hard usage. Outlining brushes that are properly soft and yet still resiliant can be difficult to get. It will be up to the rosemaler to select fine quality brushes and see to it they stay that way by good care. It can be justly said that the best way to appreciate a good brush is to try a bad one.

Whether you are buying round or flat brushes, be sure to test each one individually. Ask for a glass of water and wet the brush thoroughly.

Shake the water out with a quick flick of the wrist and observe if it forms a point or edge (if it is a flat brush) naturally. Be sure to draw the brush across a piece of paper to see if it is resiliant and springs back when withdrawn from the paper. This snap in a brush is extremely important in rosemaling, as a responsive brush produces good, clean endings of strokes. When drawing the brush over the paper, also notice if the hairs return to place after spreading the brush out to its widest span. The brush must return to a fine point with no hairs protruding at the end of the stroke. If the brush does not come up to expectation, forget it and try another. Often only one or two brushes out of ten that look alike when first offered will measure up the standards needed for a quality rosemaling brush. Remember that camel's hair or bristle brushes are much too inflexible for rosemaling; do not try to save money by buying them.

It is interesting to know that the old Norwegian rosemalers made their own brushes, and we can see from the fine lettering and outlining that these brushes were of wonderful quality. They were thicker than those manufactured today, had good body, and tapered to an extremely fine point.

SUPPLIES FOR ADVANCED ROSEMALERS AND TEACHERS

If you have been rosemaling for quite a while, you may find that it is the joy of your life. You may also discover that you are selling some of your work, and if so you may be using your paints and brushes every day. For those who paint regularly and are proficient at rosemaling the following additional supplies will prove a worthwhile investment and helpful in many ways.

Additional Supplies:
Piece of string
Liner stick, metal or wooden
Whiting—1# box
Pint jar and rice
Silicoil brush cleaning tank

Additional Colors:
Cadmium Red—deep
Alizarin Crimson
Green Earth
Green Umber
Paynes Gray
Cadmium Yellow—light
Ultramarine Blue

Additional Brushes:
Liners
Quills
Beveled brushes (Filberts)
Special brushes for background painting

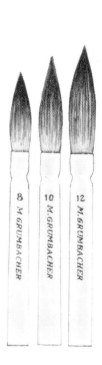

Figure 56.
Quills

"Knife" liners

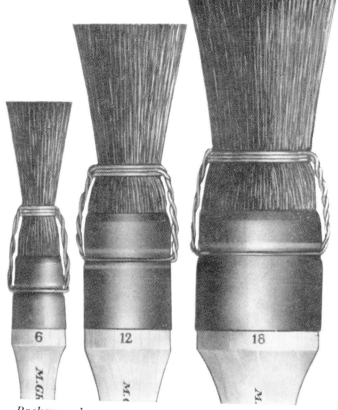

Background or
"glue" brushes

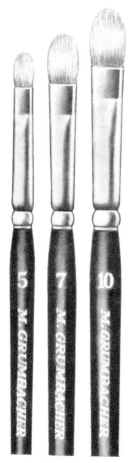

Filberts

Style	Company	Series No.	Recommended Sizes	Hair Type
Liners				
—regular	Langnickel	388	1, 2	Camel Hair
—knife	Grumbacher	1010	1, 2	Camel Hair
Quills	Grumbacher	297G	8, 10, 12	Camel Hair
—handles separate				
	A. Langnickel with wire bridles	1391	same	Camel Hair
Filberts	Grumbacher	1859	5, 7, 10	Red Sable
Background brushes —called "glue" brushes	Grumbacher	3380 —with wire bridles	12, 24	Bristle

The string is used with your chalk to divide a surface to be painted into equal sections so that symmetrical designs may be drawn on accurately. This will be explained in detail in Chapter 7. The liner stick is a metal or wooden rod with a rubber tip on either end that is used to support the hand and arm while marking a long curved or straight stroke with a brush. Whiting is a fine powder made from ground stone and is also known as ground silicate. It is rubbed on the back of a design and the excess is then shaken off. The design is laid powdered-side-down on the area to be painted, and the lines are traced over with a pencil. The powdered whiting leaves a white line wherever the pencil has traced. If you partially fill a pint jar with rice, you will find it is a handy holder for the brushes you are using. The rice will keep the brushes separated by holding them upright.

The advanced student, because of his interest in exploring new styles and the fact that he is more productive, will of necessity have many more brushes than the beginner. The ideal situation when rosemaling is to have one brush for each color. The work will proceed much faster if this is done because the painter will not have to stop to clean his brush between strokes. It is quite disruptive to be changing colors on your brush when you are creating a design. This can cause you to lose the rhythm and flow of the work.

There are two basic types of liner brushes. One is very long and thin, and the other, the "knife" liner, is wider, with a bevel on one edge and is more commonly used. These brushes are used to draw the long, straight strokes mentioned in connection with the liner stick. They are also used for particularly long outlining strokes. The quills are thick, round brushes used for doing the trim around moldings and the raised edges on recessed areas. They are inexpensive and save a great deal of time, as they allow the rosemaler to paint both sides of a molding at once and can do a great variety of widths and edges. They also save time on lining. Simply mark off the line you wish to follow with a pencil or liner brush and follow it down with a quill to have a perfect edge.

The special round background brushes are much larger than ordinary rosemaling brushes; they are common in Norway, but are seldom used in the United States. They are wound with a string or wire bridle tightly around the ferrule—the part of the brush where the hairs meet the handle. As the brush wears down, the original length may be maintained by unwinding part of the string or unsnapping part of the wire. As you unwind the string or wire, be sure to cut off the cork inside so that it is not longer than the wire or string. Because of the fine quality of the hairs in these brushes they leave no ridges, and a background painted with one of them is unusually smooth. They are useful for painting on edges, following a pencil line, and painting the largest strokes on ceiling designs.

They also have the wonderful quality of not dripping paint. A #6 is best for small objects; a #12 for larger items, and a #18 or larger for areas such as big chests or doors. If these brushes are unobtainable, as they may well be, a good quality flat bristle or nylon brush, from 1½″ to 3″ wide, will be perfectly suitable for painting backgrounds.

Filberts are basically flat brushes with the top edges beveled down on either side to give them a more rounded appearance. They have several advantages which some rosemalers prefer. For instance, when painting wet on wet they blend colors well from one to another, giving the painting a softer look, and since the top edge is rounded there is less chance that hairs will split out and give the strokes a ragged line. The main disadvantage of Filberts is that they only work well on larger surfaces, so they are not commonly used for rosemaling.

The sizes given for the special brushes do not have to be rigidly adhered to. A variance in size, up or down the size scale for brushes, is perfectly all right. Choose the brush sizes that please you best. It will probably not be necessary to have more than one each of the liner brush and the quills.

CARE OF BRUSHES

You will find that one of the hardest things to do when learning to rosemale is to take care of a good brush, and the easiest thing to do is to ruin it. The way to do the latter is simply not to clean it when you are through painting. Once paint dries on a brush the hairs are completely stiff and unwieldy. Even if you are able to soak out the dried paint and get the brush clean, it will usually fail to come back to the sharp edge or point it formerly had since the hairs will spring out instead of lying flat.

The way to care for brushes properly is to use special handling in the cleaning process so that they will retain flexibility and softness. When you stop painting for more than an hour or two, dip the brush in thinner and wipe it firmly on a piece of cloth or toweling. Be sure to stroke the brush between your fingers from the ferrule to the end of the hairs. Never rub the hairs roughly against each other or twist them while cleaning, as this can cause the hairs to protrude rather than lie flat against each other. Continue to dip the brush in turpentine and wipe it off until all the paint is removed. It does not hurt to wash your brushes occasionally with soap and water. Sometimes paint builds up near the ferrule causing the hairs to separate. This accumulation of paint can most effectively be removed by washing the brush with soap and water after it has been cleaned with turpentine. With soap in the brush, massage the hairs from the ferrule out toward the tip to get rid of stubborn paint. Be sure you wash the soap completely out of the brush afterward.

After the brushes have been thoroughly cleaned with either turpentine or turpentine plus soap and water, lubricate them with vaseline. When applying vaseline, be sure to work it down into the hairs and bring the brush back to its natural point or edge. Do not neglect to lubricate your brushes each time. This is the most essential factor in taking care of your equipment. If you plan to leave your work for less than an hour or two, clean the brushes with turpentine and dip them in linseed oil before laying them aside. If you wish to spend some money on a special cleaner, the Silicoil brush cleaning tank does a good job of loosening paint and causing it to fall out of the hairs. It not only makes cleaning easier and eliminates the need for turpentine and soap after each cleaning but helps keep the brushes soft. This cleaner may be purchased in most art supply stores.

Never lay your brushes loosely in a paint box, as they will roll onto their tips if the container is not kept level. Any continued pressure on the tips of the hairs will bend them, and the brushes will be rendered unusable. This is particularly true of the long thin outlining brushes. Some of the best ways to store brushes to keep them in good shape are as follows: 1) Use a newspaper or brown paper and roll your brushes together tightly in it. Fold the extra ends of the paper under and lay the package flat. This seems to be the easiest and least expensive method. 2) Buy a commercial brush holder, which is usually a flat metal container with wire springs that hold the brushes firmly in place. It can be purchased in most art supply stores. One disadvantage of this type of box is that it will only hold a limited number of brushes and after the rosemaler has collected many brushes he will need to buy an additional one. 3) Use one of the following homemade methods devised by professional rosemalers for storing *flat* brushes to avoid cleaning them daily: (a) wire the brushes around a stick and immerse them in a can of raw or boiled linseed oil so that the stick hits the bottom of the can and the hairs of the brushes are suspended, submerged in oil: (b) punch various size holes in a metal can top. Push the handles of the brushes up through the holes and allow the hairs to hang down into the can filled with oil. These are two handy methods to save work but must not be used for more than a few days at a time or the brushes will be ruined. Too much submerging causes the hairs to stand out. Pointed brushes must *always* be cleaned daily and kept in vaseline.

CHOICE OF PRACTICE SURFACES FOR STUDENTS

There are several different surfaces recommended by various teachers, but only the most thoroughly proven will be mentioned in this book. Painted wood is the traditional and most desirable surface to learn on, but it is expensive and heavy. Painted masonite board is suggested by the majority of Norwegian rosemaling teachers because it is similar to a wooden surface and is therefore excellent for students to use while learning. This is the surface which is most strongly recommended. To get the masonite boards ready for the design usually requires two coats of a semi-gloss base paint, a similar procedure for painting a piece of furniture except it is not necessary to sand between coats. Some rosemalers find it a good shortcut to spray the first coat on and apply only the final coat with a brush. Any inexpensive, oil based spray paint can be used for this purpose.

Some teachers like to have beginners practice on acetate paper instead of masonite panels as it allows the student to save his work with ease. This paper comes in rolls and can be bought in art supply stores by the lineal foot. If you wish to try it be sure to purchase opaque rather than clear acetate paper. It has a film on one side which gives that side more "tooth," and this is the side you will paint on. Acetate paper can be taped over a masonite board to give a firm backing while you are working on it, and if a design has been taped to the board first it will show through even the opaque acetate. This method allows students to copy over a design directly and avoid recopying onto a surface with carbon. It saves time and effort but also deprives the student of learning to draw rosemaling forms by copying designs.

Some teachers have their students practice strokes on tracing paper or even newspaper; whatever system you choose, try not to stray too far from the wood or masonite surface, which will give you the most true feeling for rosemaling.

PREPARATION OF BACKGROUNDS FOR ROSEMALING

It is relatively easy to prepare a background for rosemaling. A raw piece of wood needs to be carefully sanded until it is completely smooth, with the sanding done in the direction of the grain of the wood. Any large holes or cracks can then be filled with a wood filler or plastic wood compound and sanded down. However, there is no need to fill in every tiny imperfection because it is attractive for the surface to have a natural, handcrafted look. Remember that the old rosemalers painted right over the logs used in constructing the walls in the cottages and lofts.

If you wish to have your first coat of background paint cover completely, you must prime the wood with a coat of shellac or any other sealer you prefer. This will prevent the paint from soaking into the wood. If you have knotholes in the object you are to paint, it is a wise idea to seal them with a special shellac made up of an ordinary shellac to which titanium white has been added. This pigmented shellac is called a "flat white primer sealer" or "stain killer" and comes in pint size and in many brands. The advantage to using such a shellac is that it will prevent the outline of the knotholes from eventually "burning," or bleeding, through the base paint. Sometimes the old rosemalers preferred to decorate a more natural looking surface, so they allowed the wood grain to show through slightly but not enough to interfere with the design. This more rustic look is achieved by using no primer and one coat of base paint only.

If you wish a perfectly smooth and even surface to paint on, you will probably need to lightly sand the first coat and then add another coat. On new wood it is important to apply two coats because the first coat will raise the grain of the paint and give the surface a roughness that will need to be sanded down completely before the second base coat is painted on. Most of the time it is unnecessary to use more than two base coats; however, if the surface you are covering has been badly damaged or is of poor quality more than two coats may be needed to get the surface in good condition.

Painting on bare wood was *rarely* done in Norway, and while it is now being done in the United States it goes against the tradition of rosemaling, which is to decorate *painted* wooden surfaces. The main objection is that the grain of any wood competes with the rosemaling design and the surface becomes overworked and busy looking. Sometimes one coat of glazing over bare wood can give a good effect, but again one needs to be careful since, on a soft wood, without a sealer, the grain can come through even more.

Whenever a background color, or undercoating, is used it should be applied in even brush strokes, beginning along one side of the object, stroking the paint in the direction of the grain of the wood, and covering up the edge of the last stroke with the next one.

Semi-gloss, oil based, commercial paints are used as the ground color for rosemaling. A flat paint is too dull to suit the brilliance of the colors used in the designs, and a high gloss is too smooth to hold the paint. A semi-gloss paint has enough luster to make an attractive ground and also enough "tooth" to allow the rosemaling to adhere to it. The new semi-gloss latex paints tend to be a little too flat in appearance to be satisfactory. It is also safer to use oil on oil. If you use two different materials such as a latex for the background color and then a design painted on top of the latex with oils, you are taking a chance that they may not stick to each other.

PURCHASING BACKGROUND COLORS

In order to save time and avoid inaccuracies in remembering complicated formulas for mixing each of the various background colors you want, limit your purchase of any background paint to colors that are either the nearest brighter color to the hue you wish to use, or the nearest true hue that is available. If you choose the first method, the nearest brighter color to the hue you wish, you can work with toners, which are available in tubes called "tinting toners" and sold in most paint stores. These tinting tubes contain the same colors as your oil tubes, such as burnt umber, Prussian blue, and yellow ochre, but they are much more concentrated so that they can change the hue of a much larger quantity of paint.

If you decide to work from the closest colors to true hues that you can find, you will be able to limit your purchase of any background paint to cans of the basic color. Get the primary colors of red, yellow, and blue and the secondary colors of green and orange. Decide which colors you will use more of and buy pint or quart sized cans accordingly. You will also need the neutrals of black, white, and brown to use as toners. When you buy these colors they will appear extremely vivid. This is as it should be because you want to work with the true hues just like those you have in your oil tubes. Learn to mix the background colors as you would your tube paints by applying the same rules as those in Chapter 4 on color. This way you will never forget how you have done it or fail to come up with good Norwegian ground colors.

Frequently you will have to buy a high-gloss enamel in order to get these true hues. In this case a gloss modifier must be added to kill the shine. There is no formula for how much of it to use because each paint brand varies and each situation must be worked out individually. A gloss modifier can be bought in paint stores in pint sized cans.

MIXING BACKGROUND COLORS

In mixing background colors it is convenient to keep extra containers such as coffee cans on hand because any can of paint you buy will be full to start with and will have to be transferred to a larger container. Reserve part of the original color you have mixed in a small can so that you can check the change you have made in mixing. This reserve can also be used for lines and banding if needed. Keep mixing sticks on hand. You can usually get these from a lumber yard. Be sure they are considerably longer than the depth of the largest container, to avoid covering your hands with paint.

Paint cans, no matter how tightly sealed, allow some air in, which will usually cause a skin to form on the surface of the can. This skin will preserve the paint underneath. Leave it on, and when you need some more paint from a particular can just cut it around the edge with a knife and remove it. If you open a paint can and are planning to use it again within a few days, it helps to pour some water on top of the paint where it will stay and keep the paint fresh. Just pour the water off when you want to use the paint. If the paint is lumpy, strain it through an old nylon stocking into another can.

"WET-ON-WET" BACKGROUND PREPARATION

In Telemark painting the background is prepared with what is called a "wet-on-wet" surface. In using this type of technique the painted background area to be decorated is first rubbed with a mixture of linseed oil and turpentine to make the surface seem "wet." Then when the "wet" oil paint colors which comprise the design are painted on this moist surface they flow on smoothly and more thinly than they would over a dry surface. This technique was especially associated with the old Telemark painters and is one of the secrets of transparent painting.

To paint "wet-on-wet," rub the surface with a rag dipped in linseed oil and turpentine. Be sure that it is evenly coated but not really "wet" in the sense that there should not be a great deal of moisture on the board. Too much oil and turpentine will run down the board and cause the rosemaling to run as well.

Just a word of caution at this point: rags filled with oil and turpentine are extremely dangerous from a combustion standpoint. *Never* throw them into a wastebasket. The safest thing to do is burn them up or to pour water on them. At the very least, spread them out to dry and then dispose of them in an outdoor container.

PREPARATION OF THE PALETTE

The way you set up your palette will be a real aid to your painting. Choose the colors you wish to use and arrange them around the edge of the palette in groupings of related colors. Estimate how much of each individual color you will be using and squeeze it onto the palette. Usually the toning colors such as burnt umber, yellow ochre, and white will be needed in larger quantities because they will be used in almost every color you mix. White, of course, is used in the greatest amount. While you are painting try to keep your palette as tidy as possible. Do not mix colors on top of one another or so close together that they accidentally blend. If your palette should become too filled up with mixed colors do *not* attempt to mix more colors by squeezing them in amongst the others; rather tear the top sheet of your palette off and use the sheet underneath. This is the blessing of tear-off palettes. If you prefer a wooden or metal palette you will have to be more careful not to get colors mixed together. Another blessing of the disposable palettes is that they can be thrown away when the colors are all used up or when you have finished painting, thus avoiding the need to scrape and clean the palette.

PREPARATION OF THE PAINT

Choose a color you wish to use, for example a cadmium red, and place some of it on a clear area of your palette with your palette knife. Now dip your palette knife in linseed oil and add several drops to the red. Thin the color by pressing the palette knife back and forth across the paint and forcing the oil into it. The paint will gradually become creamy and lose any rough particles or stiffness it had when you squeezed it from the tube. A palette knife is used to thin the paint at least halfway to the consistency you will finally use for painting; mixing the paints with your brushes while they are still thick will cause the hairs of the brush to wear out too quickly. Keep some of the half-thinned paint on the palette so that you have a variety of paint texture ready to be used and thin the rest to painting consistency with your brushes. Do not dip your brush in the oil; rather, take some on the end of your brush so that you have the equivalent of several drops. Mix the paint and oil together with the brush by drawing the brush back and forth firmly through the mixture each time you add oil until the oil is completely blended into the paint. The final result should be paint approximately the consistency of honey or slightly thinner. Do not scrub with the brush but merely use the backward and forward motion. This stroke will protect the hairs. Never pull the brush sideways. As you paint, you will find that you will want to add a drop or two more oil now and then to keep the mixture thin.

Each time you add another color, such as a toner, to your basic color, you will also have to add oil. For example, you will frequently want to add burnt umber and yellow ochre to your cadmium red to

Figure 58. Mixing paint with a flat brush. Copyright: Margaret M. Miller

make a more Norwegian red. When mixing these colors with the red, you will have to add a drop or two of oil to make up for the additional stiffness they will give the mixture. As you will learn in Chapter 4, very few colors can be used just as they come from the tube. Most have to be remixed with toners to make them suitable for use as Norwegian colors. The yellow ochre and burnt umber are typical toners for red and can be mixed right into the red while it is being blended with oil. There is no need to first mix the red with the oil separately.

There are several ways to check as to whether the paint is of the proper consistency: 1) Make a long upward stroke, such as a "C" curve, on your board and wait a few minutes holding the board upright. If the color begins to run down the curve, you will know that you have used too much oil and you must correct this by adding more paint. 2) If your brush strokes leave ridges on the painting surface that seem too pronounced to be attractive, you will realize that the consistency of the paint is too thick. Another sign of too great thickness is that the paint will drag over the surface of the board instead of flowing on smoothly, and often it will not "cover." In such a case you will have difficulty finishing a long scroll in one stroke and will constantly be having to "dab." This is frustrating until you realize that merely adding a little oil will remedy the situation. A perfect consistency of paint will have none of these tendencies but will leave the brush easily and present a clear, smooth color.

Be sure when mixing a color to mix enough. Many students under-estimate the amount of paint they will need both for background and for painting the designs. Then, in the middle of a design, they find them-selves short of an essential color. Frequently they can't remember how, or are not able, to mix the same color again. Since this can be quite upsetting it is much better to mix too much than too little paint at the outset.

Often you will want to save the paint on your palette for use a day or two later. If you put the palette in the freezer compartment of your refrigerator the paint will keep fresh for several days. When you take the palette out to reuse the paint you will notice that small dots of frost have formed on top of the paint. This condensed moisture will not affect the paint in any way. Just let the palette stand for a few minutes, and when you start painting you will mix the moisture right into the paint. If you use the same paints several times in this manner they will eventually form a skin in spite of the cold. However, you can usually still salvage some of the paint by pushing it out from under the skin with a palette knife. You can preserve your paint longer by covering it tightly with saran wrap before putting it in the freezer. The covering will help prevent the formation of a skin on the paint. If you leave the paint in the freezer for a prolonged period, it will eventually form a skin under the saran wrap. It might also dry slower after being frozen. When the saran wrap is peeled off this skin frequently peels off, too, leaving the soft paint exposed. If the paint begins to get grainy, discard it.

The best way to keep the palette from drying out is to pour water over it to cover the paint. If you are using a palette with a rim on it, such as a pizza pan, just put the water in the pan. If your palette has no rim, put the palette itself into another pan and cover it with water. Paper disposable palettes would, of course, be ruined by using this method. A piece of glass can also make a good palette and, if the paint dries, can be scraped off with a single-edge razor blade.

FILLING OR "LOADING" THE BRUSH

Before you begin to paint be sure to clean the vaseline out of your brushes. To do this, just dip the brush in turpentine and wipe it off with a rag until the vaseline is gone.

The question of how to fill a brush with paint can be answered simply by saying that the paint is not put *onto* the brush but *into* the brush. This is what is meant by "filling up the brush." The rosemaler must see to it that the paint extends all the way up inside the hairs to the ferrule of the brush. This is especially true of pointed brushes. If not filled all the way up, the brush loses spring in the area that does not have paint. A pointed brush properly filled works much like a fountain pen, with the paint working its way down gradually and making it possible to work more smoothly and for a longer time between refills.

When filling the brush, never take up the paint by sticking the brush in the paint mixture. This would distribute paint only on the outside of the hairs. Insead, flat brushes must be stroked with a forward motion in the paint much as was done when mixing a color to the proper consistency. However, this motion would be harmful to the hairs of round brushes, which are long and tapered. Round brushes must be rolled around and around in the paint to ensure maximum penetration of the paint up to the ferrule. The ability to make a long stroke without running out of paint depends not only on the smooth and perfect texture of the paint, but on your success in getting a large amount of paint up into the brush. Look at a clean outlining brush and compare it with the same sized brush which has been well loaded with paint. You will notice at once that the paint-filled brush is nearly twice the thickness of the clean brush. It is this ability of the brush to hold paint that enables you to complete long strokes without refilling the brush. Additionally, the more paint you can get into the hairs the less often you will have to go back for more.

Rosemalers are frequently careless about keeping brushes clean and the palette neat. The result of this laxness is that their colors become muddied and they cannot mix the clear yet subtle colors for which rosemaling is famous.

4
Color

It is generally accepted that color is a most important element in any folk art and particularly in rosemaling, which is noted for its exceptionally well-blended hues. Actually when you think about it, everything we see we think of first in terms of color, and this preoccupation with color influences every choice we make in the material world. A sweater, a piece of furniture, even a room makes its first appeal to us on the basis of its color. In consequence rosemaling, with its charming color combinations, can make even the simplest room or object dramatically appealing.

In Vesaas' book, *Rosemaling in the Telemark,* a story is told about Thomas Luraas, that prolific rosemaling master whose fluid and dashing style of painting left a great mark on rosemaling. It seems that Luraas was typical of many old masters in that he would share his rosemaling secrets with none and is reputed to have disliked having even a child watch him paint. One day Luraas was approached by a man who wanted the painter to teach him to mix colors. Luraas, who had a superb ability to blend color but who was not about to impart any free knowledge to anyone, quickly said, "You take some of that and mix in that and after that you take some of that and mix in that. So the town painters taught me and in the same way so I am teaching you. Now we both know the same thing. Ha, ha, ha."

This book has no intention of following Luraas' example. Instead, it will enable rosemaling students to *understand* how to mix colors. To do this it is important to take time to explore the basic principles behind their composition, to find out how each hue can be mixed and how it can be used most effectively with other colors in rosemaling. Once this understanding is reached, the student does his mixing by following the guidelines given for individual colors. There has been no attempt made to tell the student what amounts of particular colors must be added to another color in order to produce a certain hue. Instead, the student should experiment with the various combinations suggested and use the color charts to help create colors which fit rosemaling criteria.

BASIC COLOR INFORMATION

Primary Colors

The first thing to understand is that all the colors in the world can be reduced to and produced by three basic colors. These three, known as primaries, are red, yellow, and blue, and they cannot be produced by mixing any other colors together. It is from these three colors that all others are created. Red, yellow, and blue also happen to be the three most commonly used colors in rosemaling.

Secondary Colors

By mixing together equal amounts of any two of these primary colors it is possible to produce a secondary color. Blue and yellow mixed equally produce green, yellow and red produce orange, and blue and red produce violet. Thus green and orange and violet are the three true secondary colors; the three secondaries and three primary colors combined, make up the six colors of the spectrum and form the principle spokes in the color wheel.

Tertiary Colors

The countless colors that can be developed by mixing any one of the three primary colors with any one of the three secondary colors are known as tertiary colors. This name, derived from the Latin *tertius*, or *third*, means that these colors, made by combining a primary with a secondary color (which is already composed of two colors) are made of a combination of three colors. The hues thus derived will depend on the proportions of primaries to secondaries. If a larger proportion of blue to green is used, you will produce a greenish-blue, but if instead more green than blue is combined, the result will be a bluish-green. In other words, the second word of the color name always indicates the predominant hue.

Neutral or Toning Colors

The neutrals, black through lightest gray, brown through lightest ivory, and also white are a group of colors that can be used by themselves as a foil or to contrast with the richer hues of the spectrum—the primaries, secondaries, and tertiaries. Also, these neutrals can be mixed with all colors to soften or gray them. Used in this way, neutrals are called "toners," because they tone down the intensity of a hue. Black can be produced by mixing the three primaries together, but it is difficult. The grays can be mixed in the same way with primaries plus white, or simply by mixing black with white. White itself cannot be mixed with paint.

Brown is also considered a neutral and can be used as such, although it has a clear dominance of red or yellow in it. Burnt umber, which is a darker and slightly reddish brown, and raw umber, which is a lighter, more yellow brown, are both used as toners to soften a color and give it a warmer quality.

Complementary Colors

A complementary color is any color that completes the spectrum. For example, the complementary color of red is green—the color made up of yellow and blue, the two hues not included in red. In the same way, red is the complementary color of green because it is the one primary color that is not included in green—which is made up of yellow and blue. Thus blue is the complement of orange and orange is the complement of blue; yellow is the complement of violet and violet is the complement of yellow. If you study the color wheel, you will find that the complements are directly opposite each other on it.

By mixing any color with a small amount of its complement, it is possible to gray or soften it without changing its value. In a rosemaling design, two colors that complement each other used together will enhance each other and act as a foil, providing that one of the colors is used intensely and the other is used in a softened and grayed form.

QUALITIES OF COLOR

Any given color possesses four outstanding characteristics or qualities all of which change according to their surroundings. It is important to understand these qualities and the way they can change in order to be able to use color properly.

Hue is the quality which differentiates one color from another. Thus the term "hue" and "color" are considered synonymous. However, a hue name such as blue, green, or greenish-blue is taken directly from the position of the hue on the color wheel and is an accurate indicator of its color content, whereas a "color" name, such as cinnamon or toast, is often inaccurately imaginative and just commercially interesting.

A further example could be the frequently mentioned color "bittersweet," which can be any form of the hue orange. By contrast, the hue names "yellow-orange," "red-orange," or "orange" are accurate names that locate the hue exactly on the color wheel. Another example of accurate hue and inaccurate color names is the hue blue-green, which is frequently called such color names as "jade," "aqua," and "turquoise."

It is necessary to realize that there can be a noticeable change brought about in the apparent hue of colors in a painted room by a change in the lighting or in the colors of an object by their juxtaposition with other colors in the design. For that reason, it is wise to check the colors you are considering in the exact place or combinations they are to be used in before going ahead with any painting. Some artificial lights are cold and have a great deal of blue in them, whereas others are warm and have a great deal of yellow in them, either of which makes great changes in color. And all colors are directly affected by the colors around them. This is especially noticeable in a painted design. A strong hue will make a soft one look softer and duller than it is, and the painting of a neutral or a grayed color next to or on a background of a bright color will intensify the bright one.

Value is the lightness or darkness of a color. It is that quality of color that you see on a black and white TV. The value of a hue may range from almost white to almost black and will change by contrast with the value of the colors near it or the background on which it is painted. A dark background will make any color used on it look lighter than it is, whereas a light background will make any color look darker than it is. Experiment by holding one color in front of white and then in front of black to see this change in action.

In the world of color theory a light value is called a "tint" and a dark value is called a "shade." Hence the expression "the shades of night" refers to the dark values of the evening sky. A practical expression of this theory relates to color mixing. To darken the value of a color quickly, add black, and to lighten its value, add white.

The value quality of a color affects the apparent size of an object. For example, an object such as a box or a bowl painted with a color that is dark in value, such as black or dark blue, will tend to look smaller than the same object painted in a light value such as white or ivory. If the walls of a room are painted a dark value, they will seem to close in and make the room seem smaller, whereas if the walls are painted a light color, especially white, the walls will recede and the room will look larger. A color used by itself or against a light value background may seem to be fairly strong and of middle value, whereas the same color placed against a dark value will appear to be lighter in value, because of the contrast.

Intensity, sometimes known as "chroma," is the quality that indicates the strength of a color. If a color is brilliant it is referred to as intense. If it is dull or lacking in intensity, it is grayed or softened. Any one hue may have many different degrees of intensity that change according to the other colors around it. A hillside after the spring rains is a brilliant green of high intensity, while the same hillside dried by an August sun is a green of low intensity.

The way to change the intensity of a color without changing its original value is either to mix it with a neutral of the same value or with its complement. When mixing the complements red and green, we find they will produce a variety of more or less neutralized hues, depending upon the amount of each used. Equal amounts of both will produce a gray, whereas a small amount of red added to green will produce a dull green. Conversely, a small amount of green added to red produces a grayed red. The dull red for which Norwegian rosemaling is famous is frequently produced by adding green to red. You will find that in rosemaling most of the blue, yellow, red, and green hues used have had their intensity reduced by being mixed with their complements or the toning colors.

Intensity has many effects on the eye, the most important being the fact that any object painted with intense colors, whether warm or cool, seems to advance and appear larger. On the other hand, any object painted with grayed colors tends to recede and appear smaller. This is true for both backgrounds and the decorative colors used in the actual rosemaling designs. Thus a bright red trunk will appear larger than a dull red cabinet, even when the cabinet is larger than the trunk. This leads to an important rule to remember in rosemaling: *use high intensity colors for small areas only and use the grayed hues for the large areas.* A garish effect would be created in any painting should we use a brilliant hue for more than small spots of color. The largest proportion of color in any rosemaling design must therefore be made up largely of grayed colors, and the effect of the background on the intensity of the colors in the design should be thoughtfully considered before the painting is begun. For example, if you have a light background and want a balanced painting in which the main colors are blue and orange, you need to use much more of the blue: orange on a light background is usually so intense that it will come out of the painting toward you and dominate the total effect of the design. Conversely, the same two colors painted on a red background would be reversed, and the blue would stand out.

In the same vein, colors increase in intensity depending on the size of the area of their use. The more of any one color used the brighter it becomes. A woman painting her kitchen a soft yellow would be wise to choose a yellow lighter and duller in hue than the color she considers perfect. A color that looks light on a tiny color card can become much more intense when it covers walls and cupboards. The warm hues can be safely used for major areas in a design if they have been neutralized sufficiently to quiet their intensity.

Colors lose intensity when they are placed next to more brilliant hues. This is the same sort of effect we saw with values. A yellow may seem extremely bright, but when used next to a vivid orange or red it will lose some of its intensity by contrast. It is also important to realize that the darker the background, the stronger or more intense the colors that can be used on it; and the lighter the value of the background, the softer or lighter the colors must be that are painted on it.

Warmth or coolness is another basic property of every color. Red, orange, and yellow seem to radiate the warmth of the sun and are stimulating and exciting. Blue and green give off the coolness of sky, water, and shadows and are restful. They can also be depressing if used to excess. Absolute violet (a color that is unimportant in rosemaling), mixed equally from red and blue, and absolute green, an even mixture of yellow and blue, are the only two colors that are evenly balanced enough to be warm and cool, depending on the colors with which they are associated. Thus to summarize—cool colors have a predominance of blue, while warm hues include a predominance of either red or yellow.

In most rosemaling designs the colors lean heavily in favor of warm hues. Red and yellow have been combined with warm yellow-greens through the years, and even blue, the coolest color, was usually mixed with an umber that gave it a warmer tone.

Cool colors usually have a tendency to recede, while warm colors advance. If you should paint two equal sized areas blue and yellow, the yellow would stand out due to its warmth and intensity.

Black changes the character of colors to the cold side, while an earth color such as burnt umber changes colors to a warmer hue. Black mixed with Prussian blue will give a cool gray-blue, while a burnt umber will change the same blue to a warm, slightly green blue and raw umber, to an even greener blue.

COLOR IN TERMS OF PIGMENTS

A pigment is a powder that imparts color to paints. A pigment becomes a paint when it is mixed with a substance such as oil or water. For example, ochre is a pigment that comes from clay. When refined and mixed with oil, it becomes the color known as yellow ochre, a hue commonly used in rosemaling.

Types of Pigments

Pigments are classified as either inorganic (mineral or earth) or organic (vegetable or animal). One of the reasons rosemaling colors consist largely of earth tones is that the old rosemalers ground many of their own pigments and had easy access to the inorganic native earths that produce such colors as burnt and raw umber, ochre, raw and burnt sienna, green earth and Venetian red. All but the last of these colors are hues used to tone down other colors, which may account for the excellent blending techniques of the old master rosemalers.

In rosemaling we need to use a variety of colors on our palette. One would think we would only need to use the primary colors, but this will not work because we seldom can buy the pure primaries, and the mixing would be too laborious a process. With more colors on the palette, you can choose the color closest to the one you wish to mix and work quickly from there. If you were to have only a few colors, they might become muddy through your attempts to mix them to the desired color.

Transparency and Opaqueness of Pigments

Transparency is the quality that makes something easy to see through and permits light to pass through to the surface of the objects beyond. Opaqueness, or imperviousness to light, is the opposite of transparency. These two characteristics are present to a greater or lesser degree in every pigment and are of major importance in rosemaling.

The technique of painting in which transparent colors are used was common among the old rosemaling masters, but there are few who can do it today. The technique itself will be explained in Chapter 7, on advanced rosemaling techniques. This chapter will merely describe what transparency can do to enhance a rosemaling design.

An opaque color is known as a "covering" color in that it completely covers the background color. Hallingdal painters preferred opaque colors above all others. By contrast, transparent painting is often so thin that it allows the background to show through and produces many interesting effects. Preferred by Telemark artists, it was developed to a high degree in that district.

Most transparent colors, such as alizarin crimson, green earth, and Prussian blue, when painted on black will tend to be toned down by the effect of the black showing through. They almost look as though they are retreating into the background, and the black gives a deep, mysterious look to the design. By contrast, transparent colors used on a white background seem to have more highlights, as the white causes the colors to lighten and become more brilliant. Some of the old rosemalers used one transparent color on top of another. The light goes through the first layer and hits the second color. This gives the impression of light glowing from the inside because light is reflecting off the second color. The colors then act on each other as neutralizers but do not turn as neutral as if they had been mixed together. They are thus able to retain more of their own color characteristics.

A combination of opaque and transparent colors was preferred by many old rosemalers. It is rare to see only transparent or only opaque painting. In fact, the best rosemaling was and is a combination of the two because both types of colors complement each other and give a painting texture and depth. If the background was almost entirely covered with an intricate design, it still looked airy and light if some transparent colors were used. This is one of the secrets of the lyrical look of Telemark painting since Telemark rosemalers used more transparency than any other district.

When mixing a transparent color with an opaque, it is wise to be aware of the fact that some opaque colors will "drown" transparent colors. This means that the transparent color has such a low tinting power that it is completely lost, and its hue can no longer be detected when it is mixed with a powerful opaque color. This will happen to green earth, a delicate, transparent green, when it is mixed with an opaque such as chromium oxide green or a strong tinter such as viridian.

Plate 1. Stabbur in Telemark, Norway. Copyright: © Photos Norge

COLOR CHART 1. How Toners Affect Base Colors

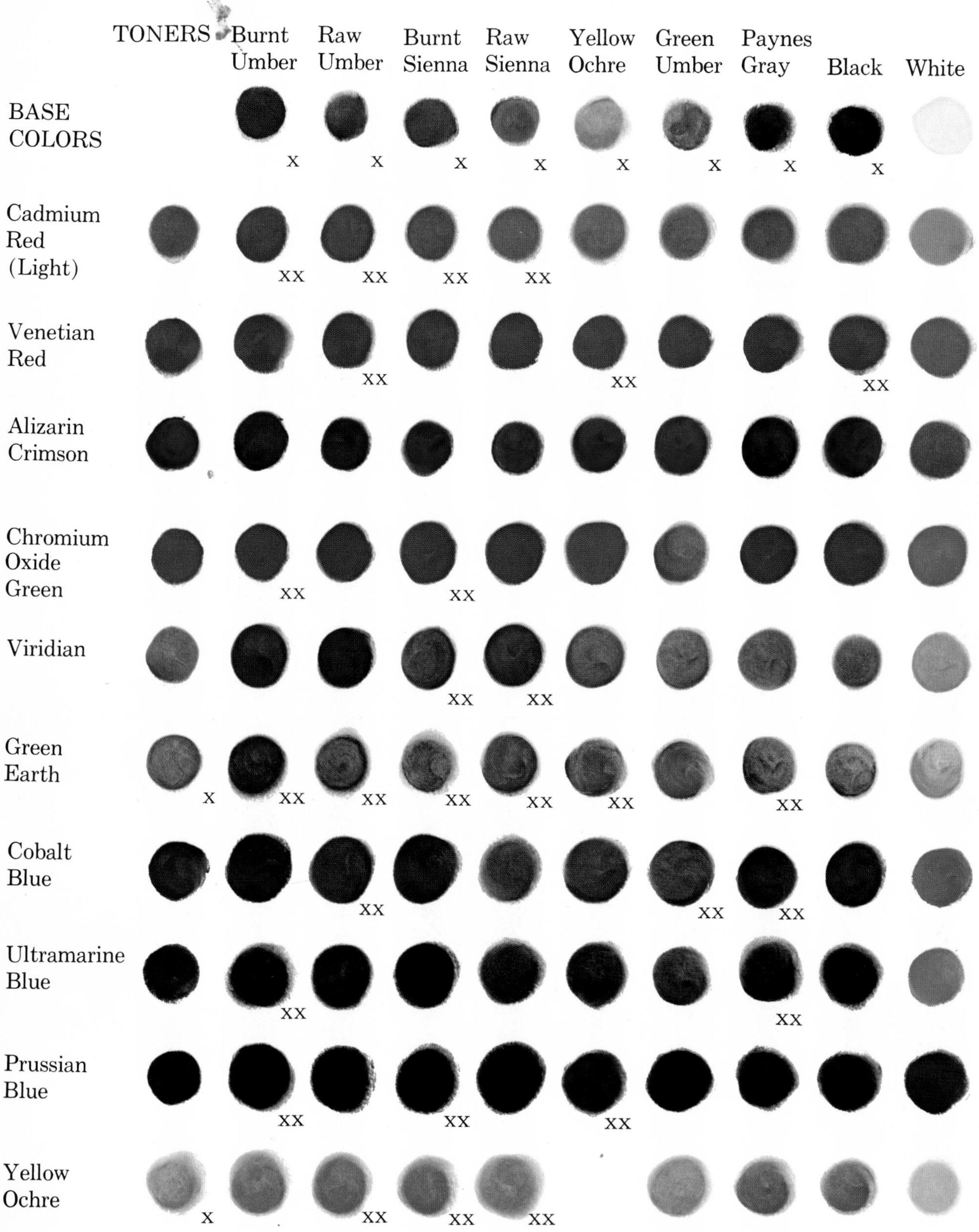

TONERS	Burnt Umber	Raw Umber	Burnt Sienna	Raw Sienna	Yellow Ochre	Green Umber	Paynes Gray	Black	White
BASE COLORS	X	X	X	X	X	X	X	X	
Cadmium Red (Light)		XX	XX	XX	XX				
Venetian Red		XX			XX			XX	
Alizarin Crimson									
Chromium Oxide Green		XX		XX					
Viridian			XX	XX					
Green Earth	X	XX	XX	XX	XX	XX		XX	
Cobalt Blue		XX					XX	XX	
Ultramarine Blue		XX					XX		
Prussian Blue		XX		XX		XX			
Yellow Ochre	X		XX	XX					

X   *Can be used straight from the tube.*
XX   *Can be used as mixed.*

COLOR CHART 2: Typical Norwegian Colors

*Prussian Blue
Chromium Oxide
   Green
Raw Umber
White

Prussian Blue
Yellow Ochre
Burnt Umber
White

Ultramarine
   Blue
Black
White

Ultramarine Blue
Paynes Gray
White

Prussian Blue
Ultramarine Blue
Burnt Umber
White

Cobalt Blue
Raw Sienna
White

Venetian Red
Cadmium Red
   (Light)
Alizarin Crimson

Cadmium Red
   (Light)
Alizarin Crimson
Raw Umber

Cadmium Red
   (Light)
Chromium Oxide
   Green

Cadmium Red
   (Light)
Yellow Ochre
Burnt Umber

Cadmium Red
   (Deep)
Venetian Red
Burnt Umber

Chromium Oxide
   Green
Raw Sienna
White

Chromium Oxide
   Green
Cadmium Red
   (Light)

Chromium Oxide
   Green
Burnt Sienna

Prussian Blue
Yellow Ochre
White

Yellow Ochre
Raw Umber
White

Yellow Ochre
Cadmium Yellow
   (Light)
White

Outlining Colors

Prussian Blue
Black

White
Burnt Umber
Black

Raw Umber
Black

Plate 2. Porringer painted by Andris Morstad, a Valdres rosemaler. The museum in **Fagernes,** *Norway. Copyright: © Photos Norge*

Plate 3. This chest is an outstanding example of Hallingdal work. The flowers and leaves, and the red background, are especially typical of Hallingdal. Copyright: Nils Ellingsgard

Plate 4. Detail of a panel by Bergljot Lunde, teacher at the craft school in Sand, Norway. Basically Telemark style but with modifications characteristic of this school in the Ryfylke district. Notice the carefully shaded two-tone effect. Copyright: Jim Jacobson

Plate 5. A chest painted in transparent technique by Sigmund Aarseth. A thin paint, rubbed in, leaves the interesting marks of the wood but covers enough of the grain to make a good background for rosemaling. Copyright: © Photos Norge

Plate 6. Door panel by Nils Ellingsgard. Copyright: Bill Lindquist

Plate 7. Downstairs in the Dean Maddens' main cottage, Binkhaven Nord, Ephraim, Wisconsin, where most of the rosemaling was done by Sigmund Aarseth. A favorite mealtime prayer is on one of the beams.

Plate 8. A ceiling painted in Telemark style at the Klomseth farm near Seljord, Norway. The artist was Mevastaulen. Copyright: © Photos Norge

Plate 9. This glorious chest is from the Tinn Museum near Rjukan, Norway. Copyright: © Photos Norge

Plate 10. Typical of the small woodenware used by contemporary rosemalers, these items, except for the brown tina, were all made in Norway. Counterclockwise from top: a blue plate by Sigmund Aarseth; a mangletre (linen mangle) carved and painted in old style; a blue tina by Margie Miller; a red bowl by Sigmund Aarseth; a tina by Agnes Rykken; a white bowl by Margie Miller; and, a plate painted by Ethel Kvalheim. Copyright: Margaret M. Miller

On the other hand, some transparent colors, such as Prussian blue and alizarin crimson, are strong tinters and will keep their identity no matter what colors are mixed with them.

To test the transparency of any color, put a bit on your finger or rub it on paper. The more transparent the color is the more of the background will show through. Notice how Venetian red and chromium oxide green "cover" the background in the color chart.

The table of color qualities in the color section will help you understand the various characteristics of the pigments commonly used in rosemaling.

COLOR QUALITIES

Color	Warm or Cool	Transparent or Opaque	Chief Uses
Burnt Umber	Warm	Transparent	Outlining, main toner
Raw Umber	Warm	Transparent	Outlining, main toner
Raw Sienna	Warm	Excellent T	Outlining, toner
Burnt Sienna	Warm	Beautiful T	Toner
Yellow Ochre	Warm	Medium O	Toner, main base color and some outlining
Cadmium Yellow	Warm	Medium O but can be T	For brilliant spots of color
Cadmium Red, light	Warm	Opaque	Main base for mixing Norwegian reds
Cadmium Red, deep	Warm	Opaque	Secondary color
Venetian Red	Warm	Opaque	Main base color
Alizarin Crimson	Cool red	Very T	Spots of color or base color
Chromium Oxide Green	Warm or cool	Opaque	Main color
Viridian	Warm or cool	Very T	Secondary color or bright spots of color
Green Earth	Warm	Very T	Secondary color
Green Umber	Warm	Very T	Some outlining and as a toner
Prussian Blue	Cool to warm	Transparent	Main base color
Cobalt Blue	Cool	Semi-T	Main base color
Ultramarine Blue	Cool to warm	Semi-T	Main base color
Paynes Gray	Cool	Transparent	Cool toner and some outlining
Ivory Black	Cool	Opaque to semi-T	Main color, toner and for outlining
Titanium White	Cool	Opaque to semi-T	Main color, toner and for outlining

THE USE OF COLOR IN ROSEMALING

The Importance of a Dominance of One Color

There is an old Chinese saying that in color harmonies "one color should be queen." The reverse meaning is demonstrated in most psychedelic designs, which become confusing because all the colors are so vivid that no single color can predominate or become the central theme. By contrast, analyze nature and see how color harmonies carry out the Chinese adage. In a landscape, soft green is usually queen, in a seascape, grayish-blue, and the fall season combines mellow shades of gold and orange. Think of how tired we would be if nature followed the psychedelic scheme.

In old rosemaling the most important colors used were greens, blues, golds, and reds. Of these, one was chosen to be queen and dominate the design. The remaining colors, plus tones of white and black, were used to fill out the design. The exception was when red was used as the dominant color. In that case, greens were grayed and warmed to yellow-green or eliminated entirely, and blues, golds, and whites were the secondary colors used. The reason why this is so is that greens are frequently unpleasant with reds unless they are very carefully blended.

The Effect of Background on Rosemaling Colors

A beginning rosemaler should develop the habit of studying each color and learning its characteristics so that it can be used against the background best suited to it. Before using any colors you have mixed, be sure to paint a sample of each on the background color to be sure that the two are compatible.

Black was a popular ground in Norway, especially, in Valdres, and the best black had some brown added to it. This was called "sheep" black, since some sheep have a similar brownish-black color. Brighter colors can be used more effectively on black than on white because the white ground will somewhat show through the paint and automatically subdue it. This means that when painting on a dark background you will usually use light neutrals that will lighten the colors in the design.

White as a ground was also popular in Norway, especially in the Telemark district. Such a ground intensifies and darkens all colors painted on it, so it is wise to use more subdued hues than you would on a dark background. The same is also true of any other light background color. The only time the design colors were not subdued to any extent was again in the Telemark district, where transparent colors were frequently used on white; their thinness made them softer naturally. It is important to remember that raw white was seldom used as a ground. Usually it was antiqued either before or after the decorative painting was done.

Red was another popular ground in Norway, especially in Hallingdal. Most colors are effective on it except red itself and some greens. This points up the fact that when medium value grounds in red, blue, or green are used, the color most similar to the background loses force, because it will blend into the background rather than contrast with it. For this reason, on a blue ground you can use a much brighter blue hue than you would on a red one, and on a green ground you can use a much stronger green than on a blue one. To be safe in using red on red, it would be wise to mix a red color that is a good contrast to the red background, such as a very dark brown-red or a light orange-red.

Blues and greens were also commonly used as grounds throughout Norway, though not as frequently as red, white, and black. Gold was seldom used as a ground, though a mustard green which contains quite a bit of yellow was sometimes used effectively.

The backgrounds as well as the designs of old rosemaling frequently have faded through the years. The original colors usually were brighter than we see them. In fact, the colors were probably fresh and brilliant at the time of execution, and nowadays we should not hesitate to use similarly brilliant colors. If the design of a piece or the area in which it is to be placed will be improved by a more subtle treatment, it can be antiqued after it is painted; that way it can be made more mellow without its strength being diminished.

Balance of Colors in Rosemaling

Just as balance of color is important in interior decoration and the fine arts, so it needs to be considered carefully when painting a rosemaling design. Balance in a design is achieved in several ways.

Distribution of the dominant color equally over the entire design so that it occupies, in various values, approximately 40 to 50% of the area is one good way to balance a design. This prevents the secondary and accent colors from gaining precedence. As there are usually at least two secondary colors, neither should occupy more than 25% of the largest scrolls and flowers in a design.

Combining warm and cool colors will also help to maintain balance. If the dominant color is cool, such as a blue, it is well to select a warm secondary color, such as yellow or red.

Repeating accent colors throughout the design is still another means of balancing a design. For instance, if red is used as an accent, it would be a great mistake to have more red on one side of the design than on the other. Since red is a warm color and warm colors project more, the eye would be immediately drawn to the side of the design favoring red. The same is true of any strong accent color. Great care is needed to be sure a design is balanced evenly in all hues.

Repeating values throughout the design also creates a sense of balance. Each design should have dark, light, and middle values in equal distribution. An overabundance of a light value on one side of a design with a dark background will attract the eye to that area of the design. The same is true for dark values on a light ground. It sometimes helps to squint when looking at a design, in order to blur the details. This will allow you to notice the distribution of values more easily.

If a rosemaling design has several hues of the same value in it, the colors will begin to fight each other. If three colors, such as blue, red, and green, are all of the same value no single one will be clearly dominant, and the effect will be to make the design flat and unpleasant to look at. Therefore, be sure to contrast values as well as lines in a design.

TYPES OF COLOR SCHEMES USED IN ROSEMALING

Monochromatic

When using color in rosemaling it is important to understand some of the basic color schemes. The simplest type of color scheme, called monochromatic, is based on using only one color in different values and intensities and one neutral, such as black or white, to give the design variety. Since this is the most uncomplicated color scheme it is the best for beginning rosemalers to start with. Such a scheme will require you to put only a few colors on your palette and will enable you to concentrate on mixing these few and getting them right.

Monochromatic schemes can have almost unlimited variations because of the range of values, intensities, and hues of any one color. If your main color is to be blue, you can mix any blues you wish in any value. You will want to have at least one blue of a light, a middle, and a dark value to give contrast to your design. A blue such as light "robin's egg" blue, which is a warm blue, can be contrasted with a cool, dark blue such as the color of water in winter.

The simplest type of monochromatic scheme is excellent for the beginning rosemaler to use for his first designs: for example, a darker and lighter value of the same hue. If you mix a dark blue you can contrast it by adding white and a toner until it is light enough to use as a value change from the original color. Push some of the darker blue to one side of the palette with your palette knife before you mix the lighter shade.

A monochromatic scheme can also use the neutral for a dominant, while the more vivid hue will become a secondary, or accent, color. White used as the dominant color on a black background (not uncommon in rosemaling), with shades of red as the accent, can be extremely effective.

Analogous

Some rosemaling designs are based on an analogous color scheme. This is one in which one primary color, one closely related secondary color (example: blue with green, red with orange, or green with yellow), and a neutral are used. If red is the primary and orange the secondary color, the shades of red-orange in between could be added to the design. A neutral such as brown will then act to tone down the brighter colors. This type of color combination is basically the same as a forest garbed in its most brilliant fall hues. The range of red to orange leaves is offset by the quiet neutral of the tree bark.

Analogous schemes offer great variety and are relatively easy to use because of their close color relationships.

Complementary

Complementary color schemes are not often seen in rosemaling since both orange and violet, two important colors in complementary schemes, are seldom used. In addition, the complements red and green are difficult to blend well together, as pointed out previously. This helps explain why blue and rust-red were so prevalent a combination in rosemaling.

GUIDELINES FOR MIXING NORWEGIAN COLORS

In order to be able to mix the well-blended hues that are correct for rosemaling it is necessary to consider the colors in two groups: the toners and the basic, or "raw" colors. (See Chart I.)

THE TONERS

As you learned before, the neutrals, or "toners" as they are called in rosemaling, are a group of colors that have many uses, such as outlining, toning the basic colors, and as secondary colors in a design. Unlike the basic colors, they are themselves neutral enough to be used straight from the tube. The principle toners are burnt umber, burnt sienna, raw umber, raw sienna, yellow ochre, white, and black, each of which we will consider individually.

Burnt umber is the most vital and most often used toner in rosemaling. It is a dark brown with a reddish cast and can be safely used to tone down any color on the palette. Sometimes black will be too "hardy," or bright, to use for outlining on certain colors, whereas burnt umber and black will be the perfect combination. Burnt umber is also safe to use straight from the tube.

Burnt umber is an excellent toner for Prussian or cobalt blue, producing a beautiful soft, greenish-blue. It is a basic toner for reducing cadmium red to a dull Norwegian red and can be mixed with the yellows to darken and soften them to a usable hue. It subdues and grays the greens, especially chromium oxide green.

Raw umber, the cousin of burnt umber, is a medium value brown pigment. It is close to burnt umber in value but slightly lighter and more yellowish in cast. Since raw umber is closely related to yellow ochre, it subdues this color well without muddying or changing the hue.

Raw umber is a classic color for toning. There is little difference between it and burnt umber in this respect except that it subdues to a slightly warmer tone. It is excellent for outlining since it usually needs no changing and possesses a nice smoothness. It is also outstanding to use as an antiquing color. There will be more about this in Chapter 7, on advanced rosemaling techniques.

Most rosemalers prefer either burnt or raw umber but seldom use both on their palette at one time.

Burnt sienna is one of the most important of the brown pigments and has a distinctly reddish tone. When used thick and opaque, it can be rather unpleasant; but it is a wonderful color when used thinly and transparently. It can be used well as a lasur, or glazing, finish because it will not muddy the colors over which it passes. It will soften and subdue when mixed with most other colors but not as radically as burnt or raw umber. It will help create beautiful greenish-blues from Prussian and ultramarine blue, and it makes a lovely red when mixed with alizarin crimson. If you add some burnt sienna to chromium oxide green, you will tone it to a soft earth green.

Raw sienna is the lightest and yellowest of the browns. This color has a beautiful transparent quality and can be used as a secondary color. It is a good toner for the lighter hues, such as yellow ochre, but it is not a powerful enough tinter to be of much effect in changing the tones of the darker hues. It is also used a great deal in lasur antiquing on light backgrounds.

Yellow ochre is probably the most important color on the rosemaling palette after white because it is the only hue that is a principle color for large areas of rosemaling designs and a vital toner as well.

It is possible to use yellow ochre straight from the tube, but it is considered more beautiful when subdued slightly. If you wish to darken it, you can do so with raw umber or raw sienna. It naturally can be lightened with white, but it is wise to subdue it somewhat with a toner while you are lightening it.

Yellow ochre is added to the greens to give them a more olive cast. It is combined with the reds to give more orangy hue and is especially effective with cadmium red in this respect. By adding ochre to any of the blues it is possible to create greens, and further toning with burnt umber and white produces some of the most excellent shades of green used in rosemaling. If an artist is adept at mixing ochre and blue he can omit greens from his palette.

Titanium white is the lightening toner and changes the character as well as the value of color more than any other toner. However, it is important when using white to remember one basic principle of color mixing: *always use another toner after adding white to a hue.* The addition of white to a color immediately intensifies it. This is simply the effect that lightening has on any color. Along with this effect white usually makes colors colder, a tendency seen most frequently in the green and red range. If you look at Chart I and compare the original base colors with the colors they become when white is added, you will notice that in every instance the base color has become lighter and more raw looking. Cadmium red and alizarin crimson have become vivid pinks—colors that are never used in rosemaling. Viridian changes to a poison green. Only yellow ochre and chromium oxide green are tolerable without a second toner added. Use whatever toner you choose to subdue the color after white has been added. You may need to add white and the toner several times before the color will reach the degree of lightness you have in mind.

White is a basic outlining color but is never used straight from the tube. One or more of the toners is added to white to dull it because white, of itself, is too bright to be used pure. It would catch the eye and detract from the other colors being used in the design. This is true not only for outlining but also when white is being used as a primary or secondary color in a design. Black or Paynes gray will turn white to a gray tone, and gray is an outstanding outlining color, especially on black, white, or dark blue backgrounds. The beige tones produced by adding the umbers or siennas to white are appropriate, especially on red, green, yellow, or white backgrounds. Generally, however, raw umber is the best color to use for subduing white, as it changes white to a warm off-white without changing the tone much. The white produced by mixing with raw umber can be used to outline almost any color against any background.

Ivory black has a multitude of uses, the most important of which is outlining. However, like white, black is an extremely powerful color and usually requires toning. It can be used full strength against an extremely dark background, but under any other circumstances it should be modified with one of the browns or blues so that it is not as stark. Ivory black is preferred by rosemalers because it is considered a warm black, whereas lamp black is an extremely cold and penetrating color.

This is not to say that ivory black is a warm color. One of its greatest functions is to change other colors to the cold side. In this respect it is used a great deal with the blues to produce several good, cool Norwegian blues, it is especially attractive with cobalt and Prussian blue.

Black has interesting effects on the basic greens, yellows, and reds, as well as the blues. The greens such as viridian and chromium oxide green become darker and more subdued when black is added to them, and green earth tends to be drowned by black. Yellow mixed with black changes to green, the shade of green depending on the yellow. It can be a raw green if a bright cadmium yellow is used, and in this case the green will have to be toned down with another color, such as raw umber. Black with red, especially cadmium red, creates a darker, more royal red. This is a color sometimes used in rosemaling on a secondary basis.

Black is most important in outlining, and when mixed with white it creates the grays. Two equally fine colors for outlining are black combined with raw umber to produce a brownish-black and black combined with Prussian blue to give a midnight blue. Both these colors weaken the starkness of black and are excellent against a medium background. Since blue is the color closest to black in value, the addition of black to the different blues will produce various shades of midnight black that are excellent for outlining.

Another important fact about black mixing is that it is used to get a clear dark color as well as to subdue and change colors. However, it does have a tendency to muddy the earth colors, so it is better to mix these hues with their complements or with the brown tones rather than with black.

Paynes gray is a mixture of white, black, and ochre. It is of fairly recent origin and was not known as a color during the time when rosemaling flourished in Norway. It is not of primary importance now except that it is often used by American rosemalers as a substitute for the powerful quality of black, especially in outlining, where black may be too "hard." Paynes gray is subdued enough in itself to be used straight from the tube for outlining and can be used as a toner in much the same way that black is.

Green umber is a color used by many contemporary Norwegian rosemalers but is little used in the United States, as American manufacturers seldom offer it. It is a rich green much like green earth but with more brown in it and is mainly used for lasur glazing because of its beautiful transparent quality.

Chart I shows the effect of each toner on the individual base colors. When mixing your colors, it would be wise to keep this page handy as a reference.

THE BASIC, OR RAW COLORS

The basic, or raw, colors are those colors which *must* be mixed with toners because they are too vivid to use alone. Chromium oxide green, Venetian red, and yellow ochre applied in the proper areas can be used straight from the tube, but they are always improved by mixing. They will be therefore considered in this section along with the stronger hues.

Norwegian Reds

The Norwegian reds are bright, festive colors that are hard to live with if used extensively in a design. On the other hand, rosemaling is more famous for its reds and blues than for any other colors. The term "Norwegian red" is synonymous with a rust-red that leans slightly more toward an orange than a true red tone.

Basic reds change drastically when mixed with white. Cadmium red and alizarin crimson become bright pinks and Venetian red, a muddy salmon-pink. Therefore, the best way to lighten the reds is to use ochre, which will both warm and subdue them at the same time. If you feel that ochre is making your red more orange than you want you can use white as a lightener, but it must be used at least half-and-half with ochre to kill the intensity of the white. Another way to lighten a red is to use a lighter and warmer red. For example, Venetian red can be lightened with cadmium red, which is a lighter and more brilliant shade of red. Conversely, Venetian red can darken cadmium red with its deeper tone and heavy opaqueness.

The reds, especially alizarin crimson, tend to disappear into a dark background, whereas they spring forward with commanding brilliance from a light background.

Cadmium red (light) is the favorite red to mix to obtain a Norwegian red. As you can see on color chart I, it is a hue that has an orange cast and usually needs to be mixed with an umber to produce a good Norwegian red.

The usual method for mixing a Norwegian red is to begin with cadmium red (light) as the base color. To subdue it, add any green, since green, as its complement, will tone red down. To give the red a more rust cast, a toner such as burnt umber can be added; it will then not be necessary to use a green. If you want a lighter and slightly more orangy red, yellow ochre should be added cautiously.

Cadmium red (light) mixed with some alizarin crimson will give a brighter red, whereas mixing it heavily with yellow ochre will immediately change it to orange. If black is added to cadmium red, it will cool off the red and make it a more royal color. However, with this red and black combination care must be used to avoid muddying the red with too much black. If this should happen it is possible to brighten up the red with some alizarin crimson.

Cadmium red (deep) is a color close in tone to alizarin crimson but which is much more opaque. Mixed with Venetian red, it makes a good dark red with a little more brilliance than if you just used Venetian red straight. It is a color that is not relied upon heavily by most rosemalers, but it adds variety to the reds and can give some lovely effects, especially on light backgrounds.

Venetian red is an extremely opaque color that is quite close to a Norwegian red as it comes from the tube. Despite this fact, it is rarely used as a dominant color in a design; it is extremely heavy and does not possess the glow that is desirable for a Norwegian red because it is too brown in tone. This dullness can be corrected somewhat by adding ochre and alizarin crimson. A better Norwegian red can be obtained by using Venetian red as the base color and adding some cadmium red and alizarin crimson.

Alizarin crimson is used in rosemaling mainly for accent or as a secondary color to give emphasis to a design that is composed mainly of subdued colors such as grays, off-whites, or dull greens. Also, as mentioned before, it is frequently used to brighten the other reds or to add brilliancy to an overly subdued red. In this respect it will improve a red that has been muddied through incorrect mixing.

Norwegian Yellows

Yellow, while not used as much as red and blue in rosemaling, is still an important color. It is the color closest to white and usually has a stimulating effect on the eye. Because of its near relationship to white it can be used more intensely on a light background, but it should be subdued before being painted on a dark background, where it will show up vividly. The mixing of the yellows is relatively simple because the primary yellow, yellow ochre, is a good color as it comes from the tube and needs little modifying to be acceptable as a rosemaling color.

Yellow ochre, as stated before, is one of the most versatile colors in rosemaling since it is a main toner as well as a base color. For a light yellow, simply add white, and if you want the ochre more brilliant add a cadmium yellow to it. You can add either the siennas or umbers to yellow ochre to tone it and have a suitable rosemaling color. However, if you add too much of any of these toners the ochre will begin to take on a greenish cast, unless raw umber is used, too.

Black added to ochre will make a mustard yellow. If your yellow turns too brown, add a little red to bring the tone back. Yellow ochre mixed with the blues produces many lovely greens.

Cadmium yellow is a color of such high intensity that it is rarely used in rosemaling except to give added brilliance to other yellows. A rich orange-yellow comes from adding burnt sienna to cadmium yellow. Combining it with black produces a soft mustard. It is especially effective when painted against a soft yellow or cream colored background and is more adaptable to modern homes since it was seldom used in a traditional sense.

Norwegian Blues

Blue has always been the most popular color in rosemaling. The Norwegians have developed outstanding shades of blue of a subtlety hardly reached in the folk arts of other countries.

The blues are all powerful colors; as with the reds, it is important that another toner be added to subdue the lightened blue if white is combined with it. Both of the umbers and burnt sienna work satisfactorily to subdue any of the blues.

One of the reasons the blues may have been so popular is that they can be used admirably with any color background. The light and medium values work out well on dark backgrounds and any value seems adaptable to medium and light value grounds.

Prussian blue is an intense, penetrating color that is the mainstay for mixing the warm blues preferred in rosemaling. It is highly transparent and leans toward the green, which gives it a warm range of values.

There are several ways to get the warm greenish-blue Norwegians love. One is to add chromium oxide green plus the necessary toners to Prussian blue. A lesser amount of viridian added to Prussian blue will also work well. Another method is to add yellow ochre to Prussian blue, while a satisfactory Norwegian blue can also be mixed by simply adding white to Prussian blue and then subduing with burnt umber. Raw umber can be used but will leave the blue slightly cooler since it has more black in it. The red and yellow in burnt sienna will turn Prussian blue more towards the greenish side.

Ultramarine blue is a color that derives its importance from its cold quality, and several of the finest Norwegian blues are decidedly cool. Unlike Prussian blue which leans toward green, utramarine blue leans toward the red. Use black or Paynes gray to subdue this color and keep it cool rather than the warm umbers or siennas.

A perfectly true blue that falls neither to the red or the green is created by mixing ultramarine blue and Prussian blue. This true blue can become cool by the addition of black, whereas burnt umber will produce a more grayish blue. You can get all shades of blue, from greenish-blue to the coldest reddish-blue, by using ultramarine blue and Prussian blue in varying quantities.

Cobalt blue falls between Prussian blue and ultramarine in terms of warmth and coolness. For this reason it is preferred by some rosemalers, though on the whole it is infrequently used. Basically, the statement pertaining to the other blues apply to cobalt blue.

Norwegian Greens

There is tremendous variety in the hues and values of the greens in rosemaling. The reason is because not only are there several good greens to mix from, but yellow ochre mixed with the blues produces some exceptionally fine greens as well.

Green is effectively used against any background except its complement, red. If green is used on a red background it will usually not tone down but remain bright looking. In this case use red to tone green; you will have a good green of suitable tone to be effective on red.

Chromium oxide green is extremely opaque and of a warmth and softness that makes it possible to be used straight from the tube against certain backgrounds, especially those of dark value. However, by itself it is a rather dull, somewhat lacklustre color and can become muddy when mixed with black or the umbers. In such a case a brighter green can be created by adding viridian, much as cadmium red or alizarin crimson add brilliance to Venetian red. The green will then be dark and rich, and gain brilliance and character.

Chromium oxide green is the most important of the greens since it is a middle value color of low intensity and can easily be mixed to either a light or dark value. One can produce nearly any shade of green from darkest to light gray-green by mixing chromium oxide green with other colors.

To lighten chromium oxide green to a soft moss green, add yellow ochre, black, and white, and if you are striving for a mustard green, use yellow ochre, burnt sienna, and white. Remember that any time viridian has been added to chromium oxide green you must not use white to lighten the color still further, as viridian and white create a violent color much the way the reds react when white is added to them.

Viridian is a highly transparent color of tremendous intensity and is mainly used to brighten up chromium oxide green. However, when mixed with burnt umber it produces a dull dark green that is excellent against light backgrounds.

Green earth is a lovely soft green most often used in lasur glazing or against light backgrounds. It can be used straight from the tube and should not be mixed with any of the strong base colors or toners as it becomes "drowned" easily and loses its identity. A good yellow-green is produced by mixing raw sienna or yellow ochre with green earth.

One word of caution about green earth. It is not a reliable color in the sense that the different companies manufacture it in a great variety of colors, so one cannot be sure of getting the same hue each time a tube is purchased.

MIXING FROM PURE HUES

Still another way to mix color is to work from the true, or pure colors. This concept was touched on when it was mentioned that some of the best reds and blues are created by mixing red with red and blue with blue. The idea is to start with a pure color such as a red, and if you want to lighten it use a lighter shade of red or to darken it, the closest darker red. For instance, to lighten Prussian blue you can use cobalt blue, and to darken it, Paynes gray, which is a bluish-black. The further away you stray from the pure colors the muddier your colors will become. If you muddy a color it is nearly impossible to bring it back to a usable hue, but you can improve it by adding a more brilliant shade of the same color. When a Venetian red turns muddy you can improve it by adding alizarin crimson.

This principle works to the extent that it will allow your colors to be clearer and fresher, but frequently you will still have to add the toning colors to get the perfect shade.

Figure 59. An outstanding example of the elegance rosemaling can achieve. In the painting done on this chest most of the flowers have been formed with teardrops. Copyright: De Sandvigske Samlinger

5
Basic Rosemaling Strokes

THIS CHAPTER is intended to give you the rules that will help you to achieve the beautiful brush technique scholars have judged was used by the finest of the old Norwegian masters. These painters gave great attention to graceful curves and smooth painting. Ability to create the same effects comes with the application of certain rules and with practice.

Perhaps at this point it would be best to say that the "rules" in this chapter have been singled out to serve as guidelines for beginning rosemalers. There have never been any written rules in as spontaneous an art form as rosemaling; the same is true for most folk arts, since they seem to lose some of their native charm when rules are devised for them. Indeed, these rules by no means represent the *only* approach. The old rosemalers did hand down some unwritten techniques to their apprentices, but experienced rosemalers, both past and present, will eventually find their own techniques for handling design, color, and brush strokes. However, it is difficult for beginners to learn without some principles to guide them and smooth the path to the point where their brush technique becomes expert enough to allow them to break these rules.

Since the highest expression of rosemaling was developed in the Telemark and Hallingdal districts of Norway, the basic brush strokes for both of these styles will be explored. If you are interested in the styles of other districts you will find that using the brush techniques explained in this chapter will suffice.

BASIC PROCEDURES IN ROSEMALING PAINTING

Before going into the specific designs of these two areas, it is well to understand and master some basic procedures common to all rosemaling first.

GENERAL BODY POSITION

In order to maintain a proper hand position it is first of all necessary to sit in a relaxed position. Do not sit stiffly over your work but try to move your body and hand with the painting, much as a pianist moves as he executes a piece of music.

You may rest your practice board on your thighs or knees, with the back of the board resting against a table so that it is upright and tipped slightly away from you. Or you may lay the board flat on the top of a table or counter and work over it standing up. In this case the table should be high enough so that you do not have to stoop over in an uncomfortable position. Kitchen counters are generally about the right height. You can expect backache and fatigue quickly if you have to lean over your work. Most rosemalers prefer the sitting position; they find that usually they can work longer this way without becoming tired. Some people like to work standing up with the board on an easel. Try all these positions and paint in the one that is most comfortable for you.

PAINTING HAND POSITION

The brush is grasped like a pencil. The distance between the fingers and the hairs of the brush is determined by the length of the curve or scroll to be painted. The reason why is that the hand must be able to carry the

Figure 60. Painting in a relaxed manner with the practice board resting on the knees. Notice that the painting hand is being supported under the elbow. Copyright: Margaret M. Miller

Figure 61. The brush is grasped like a pencil. Copyright: Margaret M. Miller

Figure 62. The brush is held so that the handle points straight over the shoulder. Copyright: Margaret M. Miller

brush the entire length of the curve, including the ending, without breaking the stroke. In other words, the shorter the stroke, the closer to the hairs the fingers may grasp the brush; the longer the stroke, the farther the fingers must be from the hairs. Experiment with this. Grasp the brush about two inches from the hairs. Now try to paint a curving line about eight or ten inches long with the brush. You will see that you can paint no more than about three or four inches of the scroll. Next try the same thing but hold the brush back about six inches from the hairs. The extra length will now enable you to complete the curve in one stroke. This is one of the secrets of good rosemaling and was believed to be a technique of the old Norwegian rosemalers. If holding the brush far back seems awkward at first, don't give up. You will become accustomed to a long grip and it will become a habit. Sometimes the brush will have to be held at the very end.

If the student holds the brush too closely, short "dabbing" strokes will show up as awkward brush marks in the curves and ruin the smoothness. One of the characteristics of good rosemaling is that, unlike conventional oil painting where strokes are often short "dabs," the strokes are long and smooth.

Keep in mind that the handle of the brush should be pointing straight back toward your shoulder or up toward the ceiling, never at a slant off to the side. If you use your brush by holding it to the side you will not be in full control of it and will lose the advantage of the clear-cut line that the brush should give.

SUPPORTING HAND POSITION

In addition to holding the brush at different lengths, use your second hand and arm as a support on which to rest and pivot the "painting hand." This is a second essential to the creation of a smooth, flowing line. Support for the painting hand steadies it and allows for its freer movement. Remember to keep your hand relaxed. Do not spread your elbows out; rather, let your arms hang down naturally and allow your painting hand to rest upon the supporting hand. The usual way to rest your painting hand is by laying it on top of the supporting hand with the little finger against the latter. As far as the supporting hand is concerned, however, there are several ways to use it; you may choose the one which suits you best.

Some people prefer to curl the supporting hand up as a fist and rest the painting hand on top of the fist. Others place the supporting hand sideways with two or more fingers on the board, and lay the painting hand over it. Still others rest the knuckles of the supporting hand on the board. Professional rosemalers often help steady the painting hand by placing the supporting hand under the wrist, elbow, or even the armpit

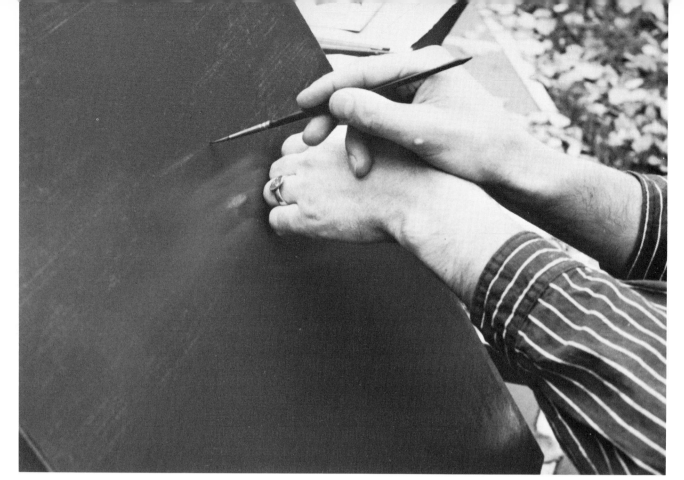

Figure 63. Controlling the painting hand by resting it on the supporting hand. The supporting hand's weight is on its knuckles. Copyright: Margaret M. Miller

Figure 64. One finger of the supporting hand provides steadying for the painting hand. Copyright: Margaret M. Miller

of the painting arm. In some instances there may only be a tiny space left unpainted on the board on which to put the supporting hand. In such a case you may only be able to put one finger of the supporting hand down, but this will be enough to give the painting hand the support it needs. It is best to stay flexible and be able to move the supporting hand about the board in different ways. Get to the point in your painting where your supporting hand will move rapidly and automatically over the board to keep up with your painting hand.

SPEED IN ROSEMALING

One of the ways to gain full control over your brush is by learning the correct speed to use when painting. If the brush moves too slowly, particularly over the long scroll strokes, it will create a stiff or shaky line. If it moves too fast the lines will be sloppy. The primary rule to remember is that all strokes should be slowed down at the end in order to allow time for the point of the brush to come back. This gives a neat ending on each stroke, as the hairs will gather together naturally when pressure on the brush is decreased and you will be able to pick the brush up off the board smoothly. This is true for all types of strokes.

DIRECTION IN WHICH TO PAINT

The direction in which to paint when working on a board or on any easily moved object must also be decided. A good principle to remember is to pull the brush towards you. Turn the practice board so that you are painting in the direction that the scrolls, flowers, stems, and leaves are growing. Painting towards your body is more natural, as your arm is not suspended in space and you have greater body control. Since a rosemaling design spreads in many different directions you will have to become used to turning your board or object constantly so that you will be working at the easiest angle. Of course, when you are painting an immovable object, such as a fixed panel, cupboard, or bed, you will just have to paint in all directions. Some amazing gyrations are performed by rosemalers, who can be seen on hands and knees or in various other awkward positions as they decorate an immovable but tempting piece of furniture.

FLAT BRUSH (TELEMARK) TECHNIQUE

The Telemark district developed a lyrical style of intricate painting that was usually asymmetrical and blended transparent, delicate hues with bolder, more opaque colors. There is an emotional sweep to the intertwining brush strokes and an endless variety of forms in flowers, scrolls, and leaves. The outlining is done with seemingly limitless types of strokes, so that each time a Telemark painting is seen afresh more is discovered that was missed before.

Figure 65. The first two strokes, with the ragged endings, have been made by an outlining brush wielded too fast. Compare these strokes with the controlled smoothness of the next stroke.

BRUSHES NEEDED

Traditionally the main strokes in Telemark painting were done with flat brushes. These brushes are what gave this style its variety; flat brushes achieve more types of endings and thus can offer a greater variety of strokes.

The size of the flat brushes to be used for the larger strokes of Telemark designs varies with the size of the scroll. A large scroll may take up to a #12 or #14 brush. An #8 or #10 is generally a good size to use on the scrolls that are painted on masonite practice boards 16″ x 20″ or larger. A #4 is usually about the smallest brush practical for curves and scrolls. A good rule to remember is to use the largest brush you can for a scroll. Whereas a #6 brush may take four strokes to completely fill up a large curve, a #10 may do the job in only two strokes. Not only does the scroll then have fewer brush marks, the work goes much faster and is easier on the painter since the bigger the brush the more paint it will absorb and the less often you will have to dip it in the paint. After all, nobody would use a small brush to paint a ceiling when a large brush will do the job in one-tenth the time and produce a much smoother effect. The same is true of rosemaling. Save yourself work and add vitality and beauty by using the proper size brush for the space to be filled. Above all, do not be lazy and try to use one brush for all the scrolls to avoid making several dirty. If possible keep enough brushes in various sizes on hand so that you will have one for each of the main colors.

LARGE SCROLL STROKES

The long, graceful scrolls may seem hard to master at first, but they are a basic skill. Once a smooth flowing curve is conquered you will develop the confidence to go on to other types of strokes and progress more rapidly.

You may ask why it is correct to start with the large scroll strokes if they are so difficult. The reason is that they are the basic part of any rosemaling design. The main color theme in the design comes from the scroll strokes, and the rest of the design and colors are secondary to them.

HANDLING THE BRUSH

Start with the brush held back on the thumb in the "V" between the thumb and index finger, with the forward knuckles of the index and second fingers holding the end of the brush nearest the hairs. Move the brush around the curve by using the thumb as a pivot point and rolling the brush down the index and second fingers toward their tips. This is a way of starting a curve beginning at the wide, curved end. To paint the curve from the bottom, start with the brush handle on the end of the thumb and roll the brush up the thumb as you make the stroke, reversing the method previously described. Be sure the edge of the brush

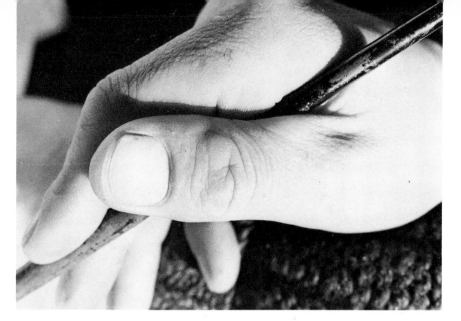

Figure 66. Notice how the brush is held between the first and second fingers in the first photo, how it has been rotated to the finger tips by the thumb in the second, and how the thumb is twisted completely under in the last. This is basically the idea for turning the brush on a scroll stroke. On a longer stroke the brush would be held back further between the knuckles of the first and second fingers. Copyright: Kolbein Dahle

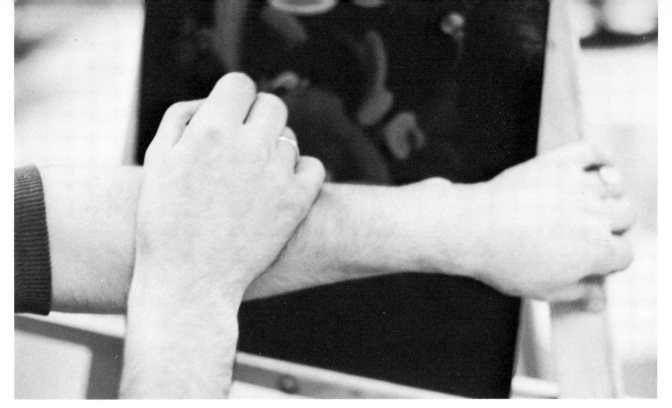

Figure 67. The painting hand gets support from the arm. Copyright: Margaret M. Miller

is on the outside of the scroll for the first stroke. One caution: *stop pivoting or twisting the brush after the most curved part of the stroke has been made.* This will prevent you from getting the stroke too rounded.

USING THE SUPPORTING HAND

One further word on the supporting hand in painting scroll strokes. It is an effective tool in helping to achieve the long scroll strokes that have been mentioned. The stroke can be lengthened and shortened by raising and lowering the supporting hand and arm, just as the grip of the brush lengthens and shortens strokes. For instance, experiment with an 8″ or 10″ scroll. Try holding the brush six or seven inches from the hairs. Now support your hand in position over the point where the bottom of the scroll will be and make a long curve. Next try raising your supporting hand and arm up, more on the fingertips, and paint the stroke over again. You will see that the stroke is lengthened several inches by doing this. A good rosemaler will unconsciously be constantly changing the position of the supporting hand and arm as well as moving them rapidly around the board.

BEGINNING AND ENDING SCROLLS AND CURVES

Acceptable scroll strokes fall into two main categories: those that are begun from the bottom, or narrowest part of the scroll, and those that start at the top, or widest part of the scroll. The scrolls in most designs will be a combination of both. Most designs have a hub from which the most important scrolls start or end, and the strokes will either begin or end at this hub.

Scrolls That Start at the Top

On a curve with a wide, rounded end, usually a "C" scroll, the stroke is usually begun at the top. In such a case full pressure is put on the brush as the scroll stroke begins; this pressure is gradually released as the brush travels down the curve of the scroll to the hub. The final ending of this type of scroll is at its narrowest part where the brush is picked off the board.

With the brush held back between the "V" of the thumb and index finger and resting between the first knuckles of the index and second fingers, push the brush strongly against the board so that the hairs are spread out and begin to roll it with the thumb; in this way the round ending is accomplished at the beginning of the stroke. As the brush moves along toward the end of the scroll, begin to relax pressure so that the hairs narrow to a suitable width for ending. If an extremely narrow ending is desired, turn the brush on its side so as to use the thinnest edge.

Figure 68. The painting of a main "C" scroll and adjoining curves. The supporting hand steadies the painting hand under the elbow on the main scroll. All curves begin from the top except the two lowest. Observe the order in which the strokes were made. Turn the page for more examples. Copyright: Kolbein Dahle

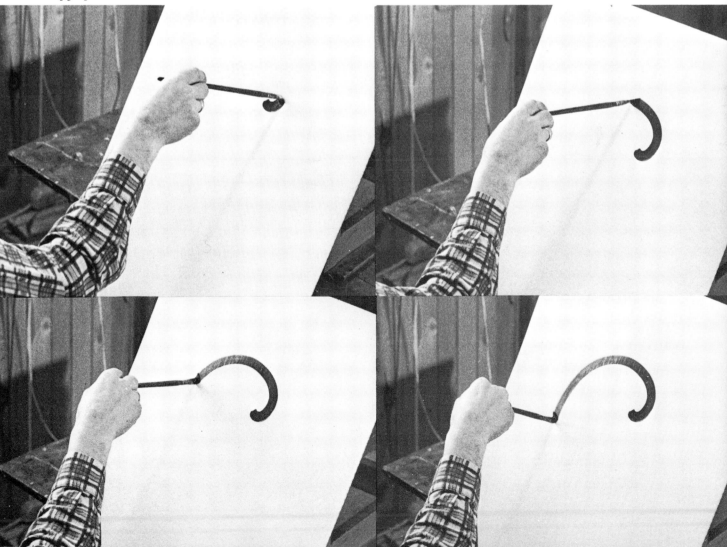

Figure 69. Two scroll strokes which begin at the top.

Scrolls That Start at the Bottom

Many scrolls in rosemaling are executed from the bottom up. These are usually scrolls that have a pointed ending at the top rather than a rounded curve.

Beginning these scrolls is quite simple. Some will be fairly wide at the bottom. In such a case the painter can begin the stroke with the wide edge of a flat brush and just widen the hairs with pressure as the stroke goes up the curve. However, in many cases the bottom of the curve is extremely narrow. If so, the only way to start the stroke is by beginning with the brush on the narrow edge and turning it onto the wide edge as the curve widens. Usually pressure is gradually increased until the curve of the scroll is the widest part of the stroke. At this point the brush is withdrawn by releasing pressure and drawing it carefully from the surface.

A professional example of a scroll or curve ending can be observed in the work of leading rosemalers. In this type of ending, relax hand pressure and begin to draw up the brush but just before the hairs leave the board the hand, fingers, and wrist must give a slight reverse motion

Figure 70. Scrolls which start from the bottom. The numbers on the one example indicate the order in which the strokes were painted.

to the brush. The resultant ending comes back just a little over the stroke itself with a slightly hooked look and gives the curve a very finished appearance. It also creates the impression that a confident and practiced hand has wielded the brush, as indeed it has.

Scrolls That Begin at Both Ends

Many scroll combinations use curves that begin from both ends. Notice the various combinations in Figure 71. The order in which the strokes were taken is indicated for each one. (The curves have been marked with an "X," indicating the point at which the scroll stroke was started.) If a scroll combination has one main curve distinctly larger than the others, it is painted first.

Figure 71. Combined scrolls which start from both ends. Again the numbers mark the order in which the strokes were taken. The arrows indicate the direction of each stroke.

Filling Large Curves

A common problem for beginning rosemalers is their inability to decide in what order to put strokes on a curve or scroll. To help resolve this dilemma, think of a scroll as having an "outside" and an "inside" edge. The outside edge is just that, the *outside* of the scroll, and the inside edge is the one that curls *inward*. Besides these two edges, there are often smaller curves and scrolls extending from the inside or outside edges of the main curve. For beginners, when there are a number of scrolls together of approximately the same size, the best solution is to start from the outside edge and work in. This causes the sweep of each stroke to cover the edge of the previous stroke taken and gives a smoother effect. Again, when there is a main scroll that is obviously larger, it is painted first and the smaller scrolls after. It is *imperative* to paint the main scroll in first so as to be sure where to put it. With flat brush technique these large scrolls are filled in from the outside edge first. See Figure 72. The numbers represent the order in which strokes are to be taken, and the dotted lines show the approximate area a single stroke should cover when more than one is necessary to fill a particular part of the design.

Avoid Breaking a Stroke

Never break a long scroll stroke off before it is completed. Now that you have analyzed the order in which to paint the strokes, another word of caution: it is impossible to continue a stroke smoothly from the point of the break. Even the longest scrolls must be painted with strokes that are continuous from beginning to end. This may be hard to do, but it is

essential and can be mastered with practice. If you find, as often happens, that you have gripped the brush too short or for some other reason cannot finish the stroke, just stop and take the stroke over *from beginning to end*. There is no need to wipe the previous stroke out; just go over it, starting at the beginning of the curve. If you try to begin in the middle of a scroll and continue a line, the trails will always show. This is not good rosemaling technique.

Figure 72. Typical order for painting combinations of scrolls.

Avoid Flattening a Curve

One of the most obvious beauties of fine rosemaling is a well-rounded curve. This is a basic point for the beginning student to learn early. A "flat" curve is awkward looking and gives a shapeless, amateurish appearance to the design. Sometimes it is hard for the beginner to recognize a flat curve, but training makes them easy to identify. Even a long, fairly straight scroll should have a gentle curve.

Note the difference in the curve between the natural look of the dotted line and the unpleasing "flattened" look of the original curve. (See Figure 73.)

Figure 73. Examples of a "flattened" curve and a natural curve. Dotting shows where the flattened curve should have gone.

Applying Brush Pressure

Along with mixing colors properly, brush pressure is one of the *most important* factors to learn in becoming a fine rosemaler. It cannot be emphasized enough that to master good rosemaling technique you must understand the control of the brush strokes through pressure on the painting hand transmitted to the hairs of the brush. This idea of pressure can best be understood if you realize that in rosemaling a rhythm can develop of its own by the way the artist relaxes and increases the pressure of the brush, thus causing the strokes to widen and narrow rapidly.

Do not be afraid of the brush. Rather, make it work for you. As skill develops you will find that you can guide the brush with authority, and the painting will become a relaxed process.

Hold the brush lightly—firm but not tight—and take a long, narrow stroke with the side edge of the brush. Now do the same thing, but while taking the stroke turn the brush to its wide, flat side. Begin to press down gradually on the brush, until the bristles are spread out as wide as possible. In a #10 or #12 brush this can be up to one inch. This technique of rosemaling causes a scroll to be filled up with one or two strokes rather than many. A clear indication of the painter who is not using enough brush pressure is the use of small narrow strokes when only a few wide ones are needed. This gives the same "dabbing" effect that results from using a too small brush.

Figure 74. Beginning a stroke on the side edge of the brush and ending with full pressure. Copyright: Kolbein Dahle

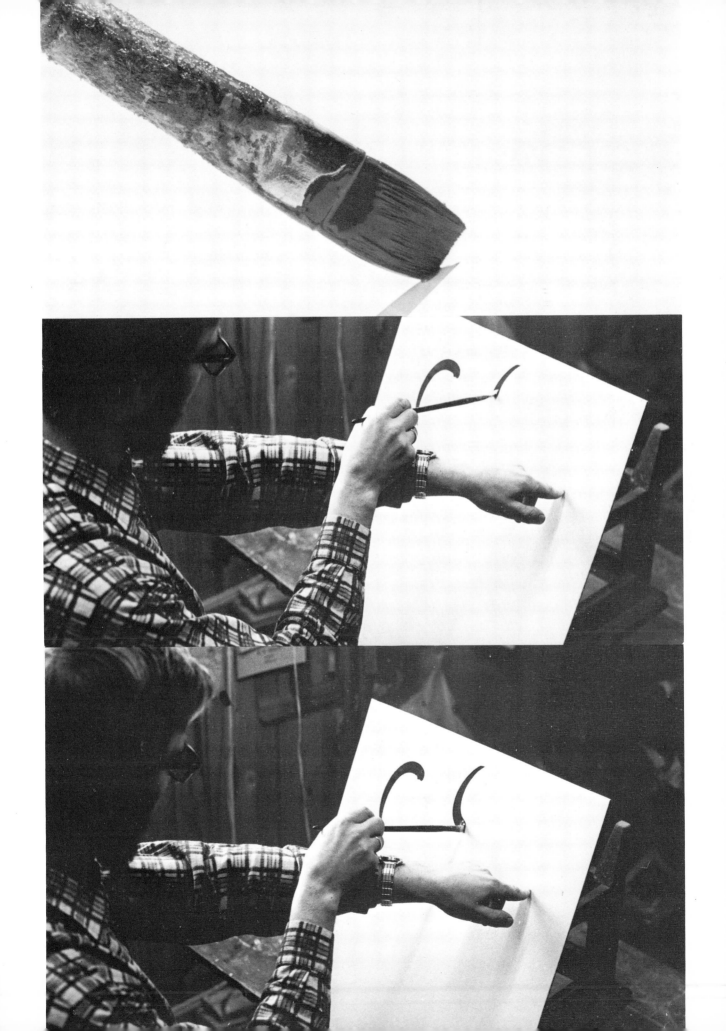

PRACTICING BRUSH PRESSURE

Possible the easiest way for a beginner to get the idea of brush pressure is by practicing certain strokes common to rosemaling.

"C" and "S" Scrolls

Two of these practice strokes are the "C" or "comma" curve and the "S" form. Both these strokes are usually made with all sizes of brushes, from large, flat, and round brushes to smaller outlining brushes. The more brushes you practice with, the more your skill will develop.

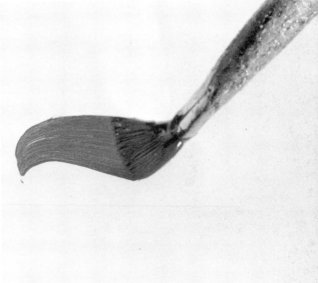

Figure 75. Brush pressure as applied to the "C" scroll. Copyright: Kolbein Dahle

Figure 76. Brush pressure as applied to the "S" curve. Notice that the brush begins the stroke at the same width as it ends the stroke. Copyright: Kolbein Dahle

Figure 78. The first "S" form is incorrectly painted. It is a common fault of beginners to make the "S" look like a written "S." In actuality it is a gentle curve as shown in the second form.

The Telemark district is famous for its use of the "C" scroll as the central point in a design. The "C" is also commonly used as a teardrop in outlining. (See page 132 to learn how to make the teardrop stroke with an outlining brush. You have already been initiated into painting larger "C" scrolls with a flat brush on page 88).

The "S" form will help you develop pressure; it expresses the rhythm of rosemaling because the stroke is made by starting with the tip of the brush, increasing pressure through the central part of the "S," and finishing off the stroke on the tip of the brush again. It will give you the idea of pressing down and lifting up the brush. The "S" form is commonly used to define leaves in rosemaling.

You can master the idea of these simple forms by painting them repeatedly and in doing so begin to feel the effect of brush pressure. This in turn will lead you to an understanding of the rhythm in rosemaling, which is generated by the increase and decrease of pressure. A #2 or #3 outlining brush is recommended for the practice of the smaller versions of these strokes.

Full or Half Circle Strokes

To paint a full circle, put the brush down straight on, using the wide width. Roll the brush around between the thumb and first two fingers, keeping full pressure on for the entire stroke. As the stroke is completed, bring the brush in toward the center of the circle and then pick it up off the board. A half circle is painted the same way, except not as much pressure is used at the beginning and end of the stroke. Both these strokes are extremely common in all styles of rosemaling, particularly for the hubs and centers of flowers, so it is important to practice them diligently.

Figure 79. How to paint the full circle stroke. The hand position for each part of this type stroke is shown. The thumb again rolls the brush around. Copyright: Kolbein Dahle

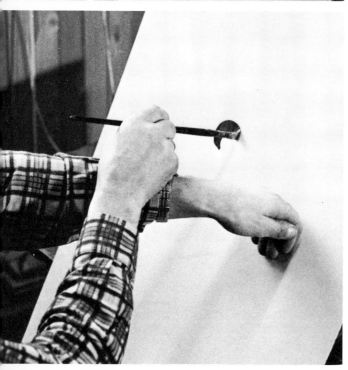

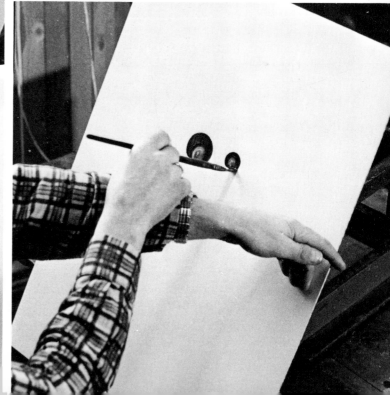

Small Flower or Leaf Strokes

One of the very best forms for getting the idea of brush pressure across takes two short strokes to complete. This form can be outlined to be either a small flower or a leaf, depending on what you need in a certain place in your design. It is a basically round form with a little extra tail coming out of the top. (See Figure 81.)

To make the form, put the wide side of the brush full on the board. Press down and make a short stroke in which one side of the brush, the outside edge, gives a rounded motion. At the end of this stroke lift up on the brush and, without taking it off the board, give it a twist so that its narrow side pulls out a little tail. The second stroke is the same as the first, except that the extra twist at the end is left off.

Figure 81. Small flower or leaf strokes.

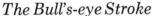

The Bull's-eye Stroke

Another stroke that you will want to practice is the bull's-eye. It consists of a wrap-around circle that begins on the outside and gradually works toward the center. It is reminiscent of the coils many of us made as youngsters when practicing penmanship under the "Palmer Method." It does not relate to brush pressure but will teach you to relax with the brush and give you more control over it.

Brush pressure will be emphasized more strongly in the pages on outlining, but it is of utmost importance to put this concept into practice first with the larger strokes.

Figure 82. The "bull's-eye" stroke. Practice with this stroke helps achieve control of the brush.

SCROLLS THAT INTERLACE

In rosemaling designs you will frequently come upon scrolls that pass over and under each other. In such a case the largest scrolls are usually the most important ones and should be painted first. The scrolls crossing under are then painted up as close as possible to the main scroll, stopped, and continued again on the other side. Any marks left by stopping and starting will usually not be noticeable enough to worry about and are often covered up with outlining.

When interlacing scrolls, be sure that the curve which passes underneath is brought out on the other side of the main scroll at the proper slant to make the curve seem continuous. To do this, draw an imaginary line through the curve it is passing under and keep the curve on this line. (See Figure 83.)

An interesting three-dimensional effect can be achieved with interlacing scrolls by painting several scrolls with a thin transparent paint and then crossing over them with opaque colors. This is an advanced technique, however.

Figure 83. Interlacing scrolls. The dotted line represents the line the eye follows through the top scroll in order to connect both sides of the underneath scroll at the proper spot.

SMALL STROKES THAT FORM FLOWERS

The word "rosemaling" means the "painting of roses" to most people since "maling" means painting and "rose" means the flower, rose, in Norwegian. Contrary to this belief, rosemaling means "decorative painting," since the verb "to rose" in Norwegian means "to decorate." People often tend to think of rosemaling as flower painting and overlook its larger scope as a stylistic type of decorative painting in which flowers add greatly to the design but are *only a part* of it. The smaller strokes of rosemaling form all the flowers, leaves, and embellishments that enrich the design after the large, basic scrolls are finished.

These strokes are not as difficult to master as the longer ones, and they have a greater variety. Applying most of the skills learned for long strokes will enable you to conquer them rapidly. The only variation to those principles is that you will seldom have to grip your brush far back from the hairs. You will usually maintain a normal pencil grip for this work.

There is an endless variety of flowers to use in rosemaling and before too long you will recognize the flower forms that are most common in rosemaling, such as the "roses" of Telemark and Hallingdal. When you are familiar with some flower forms and can call them to mind without looking at a picture, you will be on the way to designing your own variations. This is where the interest and enjoyment come in rosemaling. A rosemaler is expected to use free rein in building a design as long as he uses the forms and colors characteristic of rosemaling. Thus there is no limit to the various types of designs that are seen in rosemaling.

Progression of Strokes for Flowers

One of the problems in painting flowers seems to be the same one that often arises with the scroll strokes—the order in which the strokes should be taken. The best way to avoid this difficulty is to bear in mind the following simple, well illustrated rule: *start on the outside and work toward the inside.* It is a very logical rule and one that should be relatively easy to remember. By starting at the outside and working in, you will not smear the strokes taken previously but rather come up within them and leave a clean, smooth line. If you were to start on the inside and work out, you would find that your strokes would constantly curl over the strokes just made and leave a rough line. To apply this principle, the flowers will be divided into three categories: simple round flowers, large flowers, and complex double flowers.

At this point it would be wise to state that in rosemaling the size of the flower is often determined by the space it has to fill. A tiny area may leave room for a flower so small as to be not much more than an embellishment, whereas a large space needs an important flower to fill it. In addition to filling larger spaces, the complex or double flowers often have scrolls coming out of them; consequently the flower must be big and strong enough to support these scrolls.

When you look at the illustration that corresponds to each category, you will see that first there is a drawing of the flower or leaf, and secondly the same flower or leaf is drawn with a series of dots. Again, the dots represent the order of strokes to be taken. You will also notice that often a single petal is broken up by several dotted lines. These are petals that are too large to be effectively painted with less than the number of strokes shown.

Flower Forms

Simple, round flowers are quite common in rosemaling and are usually characterized by greater stiffness than other flowers. They often have a round hub coming directly from the stem and round petals that spring out from the hub. The hub is frequently directly in the center of the flower, and the petals usually form a circle around this hub.

To explain the strokes needed to produce these round flowers, let us *take the outside strokes first* since they should be painted first. One way to complete a stroke that looks like a partial circle and represents a petal is with one twist of the brush. Start with the flat edge of the brush and maintain pressure on it as the top of the circle is reached. Now twist the brush around with the fingers and bring the brush down next to the point of origin, so that the partial circle is completely filled in with one stroke. For a complete circle (usually the hub) characteristically at the bottom or in the middle of flowers, continue twisting the brush until the circle is complete, at which time, while still twsting, lift the brush off the board.

Completing the petal in one stroke is important to master for a smooth look. However, there will be times when you wish one or more

Figure 84. Simple, rounded flowers. The numbers on some of the examples indicate an expeditious order in which to make the strokes. The dotted lines are approximately the area a stroke would fill.

of the rounded petals to be quite large and you will not be able to fill it in with one stroke. In this case, begin on one outside edge of the flower and work to the other side, using as few strokes as possible to complete the petals.

When you have completed these strokes it will seem as though you have a messy look to the bottom of the petals. Don't worry about this because the next strokes you make as you work toward the bottom or center of the flower will come over the unfinished edges of your previous strokes and cover them up with a smooth edge.

Another way to fill in round petals is to stroke in the tops of the petals and then with one swing of the brush come around all the petals and finish the bottoms off. This method will give an entirely different look to the flower than the first method described, and it eliminates the twisting "circle" stroke. It is especially effective if you use a different color from the one you used for the tops of the petals. Again, the hub of the flower would be filled in with the "complete circle" stroke.

It is impossible to describe all the techniques for filling in petals because there are hundreds of flower variations and many different brush strokes for them, depending on the colors being used and the effect desired. The best advice is to use the rule about the order in which to fill in and use as few strokes as possible.

Don't go on to the more complex flowers until you can paint the simple ones.

Enlarged Complex Flowers

Many people associate only the simple, round flowers described previously as being typical of rosemaling. The reason for this fallacy may be that these flowers have a marked similarity to Pennsylvania Dutch flowers, a native folk art with which most Americans are familiar. However, enlarged complex flowers are just as Norwegian, have more variety, and create a lovely flourishing effect that the rounded flowers, for all their charm, lack. A simple form of this type of flower is the tulip shape that often appears in old rosemaling.

Figure 85. Enlarged, more complex flowers.

Enlarged flowers generally have a more complex appearance, and they are most typical of Telemark painting. Usually they are versions of the simple, rounded flowers, but with more petals to seemingly stretch them out—hence the term "enlarged." Use the same strokes on them as described for rounded flowers, but simply make more strokes than before. Again, *start from the outside and work in,* covering up previous stroke endings with the strokes going toward the center of the flower.

At this point it is essential to add another word about your brushes. Flowers are filled in by using all sizes of flat brushes, and, as emphasized before, it is necessary to change brushes to suit the size of the flower petal you are working on. A #2 brush may be suitable to fill in a small petal, while on the same flower a #6 brush may be needed for the stroke that fills the center or completes some of the larger petals. If a petal starts with a narrow bottom and spreads out to quite a large size, use the brush that is needed to fill the widest part. Tip the brush on its narrow edge and turn it to its wide edge as the petal widens. Many strokes in rosemaling start narrow, widen out, and become narrow again. This is where the "rhythm" of the brush mentioned at the beginning of this chapter comes in. As the brush pressure is relaxed the space narrows, and where the pressure increases the space widens.

Again, illustrations will give you an idea of the order in which to make your strokes.

Double Flowers

Double flowers are distinguished by having the hub in the center, seldom on the bottom of the flower. The various petals then appear all around the hub, underneath it as well as on top. Frequently the flower is just as large, or larger, below the hub as it is on top.

Figure 87. An example of a simple flower and the same flower doubled.

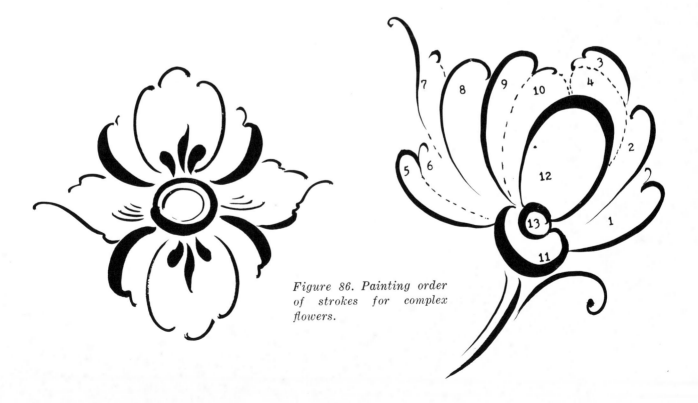

Figure 86. Painting order of strokes for complex flowers.

To paint these flowers, start on the *outside* edge on *any* side and work around the flower. Then gradually work toward the center. Because many of the petals will be upside down from the direction you are painting, you will have to turn the board around to do comfortable work on these petals.

Let us take the same complex flower that appeared in Figure 85 and turn it into a double flower so that you can see how it might look and the painting order you would use.

Stems Supporting Flowers

As flowers become larger it is necessary to make the stems that support them bigger. This can be done in several ways, the most common being simply to paint a thicker stem. You can also paint several stems to support one flower or use an embellishment such as cross-hatching to add weight to the stem.

PAINTING LEAVES

In rosemaling there is the same variety in leaves as in flowers. Many leaves are long and slender, often with curves on the end, but just as frequently they are short and round. The separate districts and valleys of Norway had characteristic leaves, which may account for the variety. In Figure 91 you will notice that the "S" form is the beginning of many leaves, all of which develop interesting shapes when the basic form is altered by the brush.

Leaves are always shown either growing out of a flower, up a flower stem, or out of a scroll or tendril. Once you have mastered the technique for painting scrolls and flowers you should experience no trouble at all with leaves, as they are the least complicated forms you will

Figure 88. Double flowers.

Figure 89. How stems support flowers.

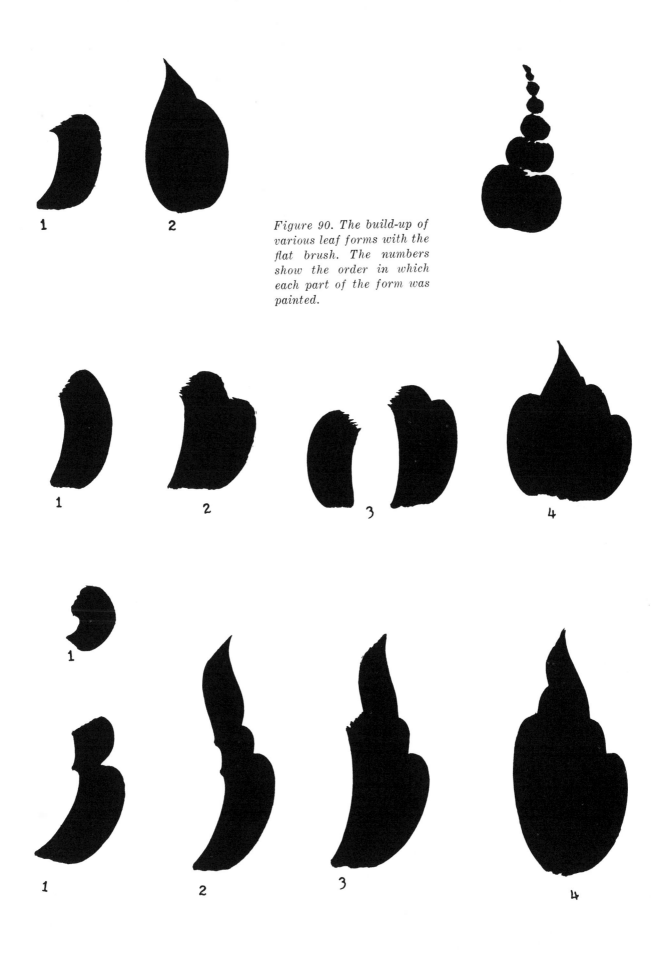

Figure 90. The build-up of various leaf forms with the flat brush. The numbers show the order in which each part of the form was painted.

Figure 91. All these leaves are based on the simple "S" form. Notice that the leaves get increasingly more detailed.

encounter. Many leaves are made with a single stroke, but as far as order of strokes is concerned for larger leaves, you can paint a leaf from either side; if more than two strokes are needed, fill in the middle last. With flat brushes the outside edge of the brush always follows the side of the leaf you are delineating. One word of caution: many beginners make the mistake of trying to twist the brush to form leaves. *Leaves are made solely with brush pressure—*a pushing down and relaxing of the brush.

Leaves with Flowers

Leaves simply seem to spring up out of the flowers they are attached to. When painting flowers with leaves attached to the outside, begin with the flower first and then add what might grow out of the flower afterward. This determines the position of the flower, and the leaves can then fill up any remaining space in that area. After the flower is painted, **go on to the largest leaf.**

Leaves with Stems

Leaves with stems are often quite small, more an embellishment to show line or movement in a design than anything else. We will not touch upon them until we come to the section on detail strokes. However, some leaves are large enough to be included in this section and examples of these are shown in Figure 93. When you paint these strokes you will generally be using a smaller brush. Remember that though these leaves are quickly painted, you must still be careful. Finish these smaller strokes as nicely as you do the larger ones.

Leaves with Scrolls

There are many places on scrolls where leaves can be painted. They a) may embellish the central hub of the design from which the main scrolls start, b) decorate the inside or outside of a scroll, c) spring from the end of the scroll, where it curls around, or d) grow from the junction

Figure 92. How leaves are used with flowers and to form flowers. In the first two examples, where the leaves are separate from the flower form itself and seem to be growing out of the flower, paint the leaves first. In the third example the leaves actually form the major part of the flower and, of course, are painted as the flower is composed.

Figure 93. Leaves with
stems.

Figure 94. Leaves with scrolls.

Figure 95. Variations on the leaf form.

of two scrolls. Several of these situations are shown in Figure 94. When used to embellish scrolls, leaves give a lively and casual look to the scrolls. Frequently they just seem to grow and grow, one leaf following another and reaching from one scroll to another element of the design.

ROUND BRUSH (HALLINGDAL) TECHNIQUE

The Hallingdal painter Nils Ellingsgard has given a clear and meaningful description of this district's style of rosemaling. He says: "In a comparison of Telemark with Hallingdal painting one will find that Hallingdal rosemaling is more brave and powerful, with the main emphasis placed on colors. It does not have the soft hues of Telemark, which create a fading out of one color to another, but instead it emphasizes contrast colors which ring or play against each other. The outlining is strong and pronounced but a little less developed than in Telemark. The patterns are most often symmetrical and built around a central point or axis (from the baroque). When it comes to brush technique there is less difference than there is in style, but the techniques are not quite the same."

By tradition, round brushes of different shapes and sizes were (and are) used for painting both the basic design and the outlining, but flat brushes can also be used, particularly for some types of flower forms such as those that are round or oval. Most rosemalers who work with flat brushes first will find that round brushes are easier to manipulate for two basic reasons: the designs are simpler, with less variety in the stroking needed for flowers, leaves, and details, and there are fewer types of endings to master. This is not to say that Hallingdal technique is easier overall. It is considered difficult by many rosemalers because of its partiality for symmetry, since to get a design even on both sides requires a high degree of skill. However, what we are concerned with here are brush strokes alone. The technique for laying out a symmetrical design will be discussed in Chapter 6.

Most of the rules and guidelines given under the heading, "Flat Brush Technique" apply to round brushes. These rules are important to follow in Hallingdal painting because the types of flowers, leaves, and scrolls are quite set and generally are painted a certain way. The basic differences in brush technique will now be elaborated on.

BRUSHES NEEDED

The #8 round brush is the most convenient size brush for using on your masonite practice boards (or on any object using a medium sized design), to fill in the larger scrolls, leaves, and flowers. A #5 brush will do a neat job on most flowers and smaller leaves. Again, the size of your design will determine the size brushes you need.

THREE TYPICAL STROKE ENDINGS

The main advantage of round brushes over flat is that they will come back to a finer point and yield endings that are usually extremely graceful looking. Examples of three typical Hallingdal stroke endings are described to give the student a basis for working on the large strokes of this style.

1. Using a wide rounded ending for main scrolls is as common in Hallingdal as in Telemark, but such an ending is formed in a different way. In Hallingdal brush technique such a scroll is usually painted with a double stroke. Carry the brush from the bottom to the top, *on the inside of the scroll,* using continually more pressure as you go up the stroke. At the top of the stroke turn the brush and go back down *on the outside of the scroll,* using less and less pressure as you go down.

2. A scroll that goes out to a thin curve and ends with a circle on the very end is easy to accomplish successfully with a round brush since it will return easily to its tip during the course of the stroke. Start the scroll with the point of the brush, exert pressure on the brush to widen the scroll and then carefully release pressure and bring it around for a distance on its top. Twist the brush around on its tip at the extreme end of the scroll to finish it off with a small circle.

3. Another graceful ending is made by exerting most of the pressure on the brush near the top of the stroke and releasing it suddenly so the curl tapers off sharply with a backward motion of the brush.

Figure 96. Typical Hallingdal scrolls, leaves, and flowers illustrated by Hallingdal rosemaler Nils Ellingsgard. The direction of strokes has been indicated.

Figure 97. Hallingdal-style
leaves and flowers.

Main scrolls in Hallingdal painting typically start at the bottom and go up or begin from the inside and work out. This is a basic difference from Telemark style, where a great many curves are begun at the top and usually are painted from the outside in.

TYPES OF FLOWERS

The charming flowers characteristic of Hallingdal painting are fewer in number than the flowers of the Telemark district and have less variety in form. This is because they are generally simpler and more rounded and have three, four, five, or six distinct petals evenly spaced. The most common ones are shown in Figure 97. Hallingdal flowers are also often formed using teardrops as an integral part of the flower, either to form the petals, as embellishments, or as a part of the central hub. Plate 3 is an excellent example of the use of teardrops in creating Hallingdal flowers.

Appearing frequently in Hallingdal designs are the variations shown in Figure 98. Notice that this flower is basically the same, but it has been painted three different ways. The example on the left is merely four cloverleaf type petals with the center naturally painted last. The shape of the middle example is formed by teardrops; the petals have a two-tone effect, most attractive and typical of Hallingdal style. To achieve this look, *paint the center circle first* with a color that will differ widely in value from the color you plan to paint the petals but which will also mix pleasingly with the petal color. For instance, a dark blue center with pale blue, almost white, petals or a pale gold center with dark green petals would be two good combinations. After you have painted the center, begin painting the petals either singly around the center or in groups of two or three. If you use three teardrops per petal the center teardrop will be the longest and the two side teardrops of equal length.

Begin the tip of each teardrop inside the circle and pull this center color out and part way up each teardrop. End the stroke with firm pressure. The center color thus blends through into the petals, to give the flower a lovely soft look. The example on the right is similar, except that a larger circle is painted first and the teardrops start much further down inside the circle. Lastly, a small, contrasting center circle is placed in the center space left by the petals.

Hallingdal flowers are also commonly made by putting two colors on the brush: for example, a dark color at the top of the hairs and a light color toward the tip. This two-tone technique is described in detail in Chapter 7.

Figure 98. Two-tone petals on Hallingdal flowers.

Figure 99. Curves decorated
by leaves in rococo style.

TYPES OF LEAVES

A word should be said here about the leaves in Hallingdal style. They are quite similar to those of Telemark and are often formed by heavy outlining. You will be able to execute them without special brush instruction. As you will see in Fig. 99, leaves can be added to scrolls to create a rococo or baroque effect. These leaves work their way up a curve in an ornate and highly decorative manner. Painting technique for these curves is a matter of learning what forms are typically rococo and then using the technique you have already learned to paint these forms on the curves.

Figure 100. Hallingdal border designs by artist Nils Ellingsgard.

Figure 101. Round, symmetrical designs in the style of the Hallingdal district by rosemaler Nils Ellingsgard.

OUTLINING STROKES

All of rosemaling is enjoyable, but most rosemalers will agree that outlining is what they look forward to the most. Outlining is where the real fun of rosemaling comes in and the area where most of the rhythm of the painting is developed. The strokes of outlining can also be the most poorly done and give away an unskilled hand at a glance.

For the beginner to watch a truly creative rosemaler outline a design for the first time usually stimulates feelings and expressions of delight. Most students exclaim, "Oh, how beautiful" as the character and charm of a design spring to vivid life under the outlining brush. While the basic strokes set the pattern and color of any design, the outlining delineates all shapes and defines their brilliance and variety.

BRUSHES NEEDED

The size of outlining brushes to be used depends upon the size of the design. Usually you can use anywhere from a #1 to a #5 on anything except an extremely large area, such as a ceiling. It is essential that these brushes have good tips that will come to fine points without showing individual hair marks and that they be of red sable. The #1 is too thin to use on large areas but does well on small objects such as boxes, bowls, plates, etc. The #2 and #3 brushes are practical for most of the outlining on almost any size area and are probably the most commonly used. The #4 and #5 are for heavy outlining on large scrolls and to give a stronger accent to the places where they are used. A #5 round brush is one of the most useful brushes for Hallingdal outlining, since it works well to fill in leaves and flowers for the large outlining strokes common to Hallingdal style. In Telemark style the outlining brushes are "scrollers," with hairs especially long so they will carry the paint a good distance. These are the type of brushes used in calligraphy to do script writing. They are longer and less full than those used in Hallingdal. This is because Hallingdal outlining strokes are bolder and thicker than Telemark ones and therefore require a fuller brush.

TYPES OF OUTLINING

Let us begin by defining outlining. Most rosemalers consider outlining to be the small strokes that are added to the outside of scrolls, leaves, and flowers to give them a finished appearance, plus the strokes that trim up the design and lend it interest. These added strokes can be in the nature of small leaves, teardrops, tiny flowers, or any decorative marks with the brush that you care to make. This definition is sufficient, but for purposes of simplification and clarity this section will divide outlining into two parts. The first will be called "Straight Out-lining" and will describe the strokes that actually do outline scrolls, leaves, and flowers. The second will be called "Detail Strokes" and will describe the additional decorative embellishments needed to finish the design, after the actual outlining strokes are completed.

Straight Outlining

To explain straight outlining we must go back to the beginning and discuss all the various factors, such as hand position and brush pressure, that were mentioned in the section on scroll strokes. We didn't need to go into this for the smaller strokes because the principles are almost the same as those used for scroll strokes. In outlining, however, the technique is often different and must be explained from the beginning.

Hand Position

In outlining, you must remember the rule about holding the brush far back from the bristles. Most of the time you will hold it in a normal grip, but when outlining long scrolls you will frequently need to take strokes the same length as the scrolls. Of course, the only way to accomplish this without breaking off the stroke is to grip the brush back from the bristles the comparable distance you need to travel up the scroll. If the first stroke does not go the full distance you had planned for it, start at the bottom of the scroll and take the stroke over. Because you have learned this grip with the scroll strokes it should be much easier for you now. Also, do not forget to move the supporting hand about to help the painting hand.

Brush Pressure

Brush pressure cannot be stressed enough in outlining. While many out-lining strokes are made by maintaining the same pressure on the entire stroke, the variety of line of most of the outlining strokes used is achieved by changing the pressure on the brush. This variation in pressure gives a design more vividness and character and produces the variety desired in outlining strokes. Think of your brush as a dancer, darting and weaving as you apply your strokes. The rhythm of the brush, created by a response to pressure from the hand, is one of the special qualities that gives rosemaling its lively and fresh quality.

Start with the tip of your outlining brush and slowly increase the pressure on the bristles. Sometimes you will paint a thin line using only the tip, then increase the pressure toward the center of the stroke (thus widening the brush), and then bring the brush back to the tip for the slender, fine end of the stroke. You may also put the tip down lightly but immediately increase the pressure, withdrawing the bristles while the pressure is still on it and the bristles are spread out. Or you may

Figure 102. Outlining strokes of uniform width indicating constant maintenance of the same pressure throughout the stroke except on the end. There the pressure is increased and the brush twisted to create the round end shown. Copyright: Kolbein Dahle

wish to draw the tip along, increasing, decreasing, and increasing the pressure on a curve, withdrawing pressure and increasing it as you make the final curl. All this is done with one stroke. These are only three of hundreds of combinations, but you can now see how important brush pressure is in achieving the graceful flow of outlining. Once you learn to use pressure successfully on some strokes you will be able to duplicate any stroke you want by just looking at it. You can now see where the pressure must go and should have no trouble copying it.

In outlining, as with the scroll strokes, it is important that you have firm control of the brush and extreme self-confidence. Do not be timid but make a deliberate effort to carry the brush on its tip and press down. Students will grasp the idea more readily if they think of this book as a teacher standing right beside them, exhorting them to vary the pressure. With this urging, you will eventually get the courage to press down and really *use* the brush for the first time. Usually it will come as a revelation to see the lovely lines you are capable of creating. From now on progress in outlining will usually be fast.

Figure 103. The remarkable variety of outlining strokes one brush is capable of achieving. Copyright: Kolbein Dahle

Speed of Outlining

It is appropriate at this time to make some further comments about the speed with which you should use the brush. While the practiced rosemaler has the skill to outline very quickly, the beginner should beware of speed until he has mastered control of the brush. Speed will come, but in the meantime make the strokes evenly and carefully so they are done properly and you can feel how the brush responds to your pressure. Be sure to slow the brush at the end of each stroke. Speed at this stage will give you an uncontrolled line that will not only look messy but be dead and uninteresting.

Beginning and Ending Outlining Strokes

Outlining strokes are invariably begun on the tip of the brush and are often ended the same way. Sometimes, though, the ending is made when the pressure on the brush spreads the bristles out. Remember, if you wish to end the stroke with the bristles wide you simply pick the brush off the board right at the point where the stroke is to terminate. Do not let the brush trail off. This is the same rule used to make the "teardrop" embellishments so dear to the hearts of rosemalers.

Remember that when outlining strokes curve, they must have the same rounded look as was emphasized for the scroll strokes. *Do not ever allow them to become "flat."* Of course, many outlining strokes are only slightly curved or perfectly straight, but even the gentlest curve should be rounded looking.

Amount of Outlining to Use

A skillful rosemaler will have not only great variety of line but will use restraint in the amount of outlining he uses. It is much more beautiful and refreshing to leave some basic scrolls without any outlining or only partial outlining. This way the outlining that is done shows up more, and the design itself does not get the look of being overwhelmed by hundreds of outlining strokes. Outlining perfectly to the smallest detail can get tiresome. Look at Figure 110 again and notice how the example on the left not only lacks interest but seems to be a mass of outlining. You must allow the beauty of the large scrolls to show and leave some areas free for the imagination. This is a principle of basic drawing. Art instructors teach their students to indicate a line by shading rather than drawing a heavy mark to show each side of an object. To do a good job on your rosemaling strokes, get in plenty of variety but do not overdo them.

Detail Strokes or Embellishments

There are hundreds of kinds of details or embellishments, and any design perks up the minute you begin to add them to it. Most overall designs, especially those with large scrolls covering the painting area, can

take a great deal of this detail work. On the other hand, a simple design of, say, flowers coming out of a basket or urn, can easily be ruined by overembellishment.

The strokes of a great percentage of details are the same as the outlining strokes you have already mastered. Take a look at a book containing color plates of rosemaling and you will see that you already know how to paint most of the details. This section will illustrate and describe the teardrop stroke and the most useful details and their variations.

The Teardrop Stroke. This is the one stroke most common to all types of peasant painting. Pennsylvania Dutch, Bavarian, Early American, Norwegian, Swedish, and Austrian decorative painting all use the teardrop stroke frequently. A characteristic of rosemaling that causes it to differ from the others is the great variety in size and length of teardrop strokes it uses.

To make the teardrop stroke, place the tip of your brush on the board and draw it toward you with increased pressure. When it is the desired length and thickness, lift the brush off the board evenly. On your first attempts make the stroke straight; when you have mastered it that way, try curving it. When you have finished curving it, you will see that it is the old familiar stroke you used with heavy brush pressure in outlining. You will also notice in Fig. 106 that the teardrop can be very long and tapering or quite short and thick. It can also be used for a multitude of tasks, including making flowers and leaves.

Hallingdal style makes more extensive use of the teardrop, so if you have already mastered that stroke you have merely to familiarize yourself with Hallingdal details and practice them until your strokes are sure and well done.

Figure 105. The teardrop made with a flat brush.

Figure 106. Variations on the teardrop. All these strokes were made with a no. 2 outlining brush.

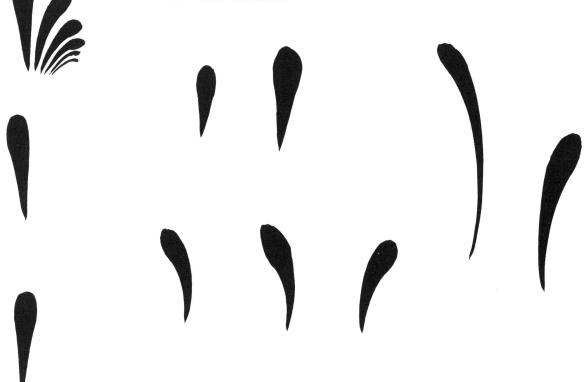

Figure 107. Characteristic Hallingdal detail strokes.

Figure 108. Useful detail strokes.

Useful Detail Strokes. The strokes shown in Figure 108 should now become easier with practice. As stated before, practice is the clue to making your strokes look as professional as those illustrated.

A common embellishment in rosemaling is cross-hatching. This criss-crossing of fine lines is used mainly to decorate the hubs of flowers and to fill in spaces to tie together the outside of symmetrical designs. When you crosshatch, be sure you make all the strokes quite fine so the background color shows through. Also be sure that the strokes of cross-hatching are clear, straight, and of an equal distance from each other, so the result will be neatly done.

Figure 109. Examples of how to use crosshatching.

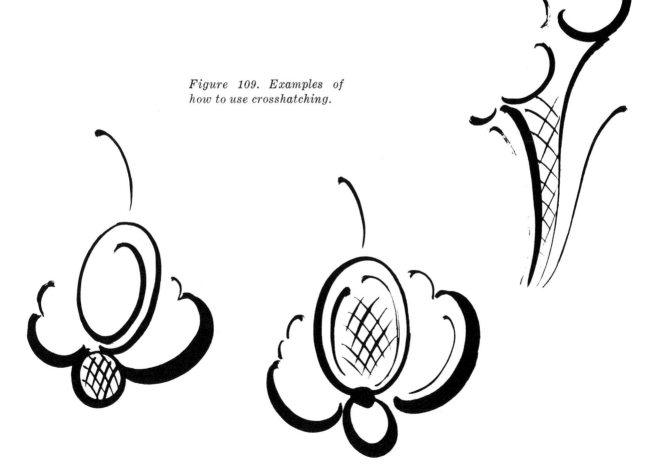

The dotting effect frequently used as a detail is made by using a quantity of paint on the tip of the brush so that it looks as though it is ready to drip. Press the tip lightly onto the board and your dot will be perfectly round. This will be most distinctive and professional as compared to irregular dots that are the mark of the amateur. To make large, round dots, give the brush a little sideways movement to spread out the paint.

VARIETY IN OUTLINING

Variety in outlining is also achieved through the handling of strokes.

Variety of Individual Strokes

The variety of individual strokes should be simple to understand since it has just been discussed in the preceding paragraphs. It is the result of increasing or relaxing pressure on the brush. The point to be stressed is that in rosemaling this variety of stroke gives the design great character and interest. It would be quite monotonous if all strokes were of the same width and shape. The skill of the rosemaler is in direct proportion to the amount of variety he can get in his strokes.

Figure 110. Variety in outlining can best be illustrated by showing a leaf form with boring repetition of strokes contrasted with a leaf having variety in length of stroke and thickness of line. A flower and scroll design is shown in the same manner.

Figure 111. Details formed from dots.

Variety in Relationship of Strokes to Each Other

Not only should there be variety in the strokes themselves, but strokes next to each other should be sufficiently varied to add interest to the design. For instance, a large scroll may have fairly heavy outlining strokes enclosing it. If this same scroll has outlining strokes within it to add interest to the scroll, they should not be of the same weight and length as those enclosing it. Strokes all of the same kind are boring. However, if the strokes are varied by plain thin strokes next to thick and long next to short, the scroll will have great originality. Figure 110 shows the tremendous difference in outlining strokes that can be achieved with the same brush in the hands of a fine rosemaler.

Variety in Outlining Depending on Color

The weight or heaviness of the outlining strokes you use will vary not only with the type of design but with the colors used. On bold, opaque colors the thickness of the outlining strokes is greater than it would be with a lighter design where you must be careful to make them more delicate. Do not confuse the weight of the outlining strokes with the amount of outlining strokes used in a design. Weight refers to the thickness of the outlining strokes only. If you notice the differences between Hallingdal and Telemark outlining, you will see immediately that the brighter colors and simpler designs of Hallingdal can carry a heavier type of outlining stroke, whereas Telemark painting, which is more open, with delicate, transparent colors, takes a lighter outlining touch.

Figure 112. A simple border pattern.

6
Creating Original Designs

A GOOD ORIGINAL DESIGN in rosemaling is a dynamic and lyrical movement of lines that combines scrolls, leaves, and flowers in a well-constructed pattern. This pattern must be well suited to the area it is to cover.

HISTORIC VERSUS PRESENT DAY DESIGNING

In the olden days the designs created by the finest rosemalers were usually so individual that without seeing the signature one could tell who had painted a particular piece. The way a piece was painted sometimes even told what mood the artist was in and what stage he had reached in his painting skill. Even more dramatically a painter showed his character in his designs. That Thomas Laaras of Telemark, the famous rosemaling master mentioned earlier, was a flamboyant person shows clearly in the bold sweeps of his work.

The style of painting within the various districts of Norway often represented the characteristics of the area. For example, Telemark designs have a restlessness evident not only in the painting done on the walls and ceilings of that district but even on smaller items. In those days there was little emphasis on technical perfection, nor has traditional rosemaling ever been a repetitious copying of what was done before. Rather, its emphasis was placed on originality of design, with style and flair getting high priority.

Today great importance is placed on perfection of strokes and the use of copying to achieve the same kinds of forms and types of designs as those executed by the old masters. For this reason rosemaling has tended to stagnate rather than reach forward with the distinctive original designing that once made it the greatest of the painted peasant folk arts. There is nothing wrong with copying the old masters to learn technique, but there should be room for new experiments to advance the "state of

138

Figure 113. Lars Sataφyen painting a panel using wet-on-wet technique.
Copyright © Photos Norge

the art." Many modern rosemalers feel there is nothing they can add to an already highly developed art form without taking away from its recognized style. The old painters did not worry about this problem. They were creating the style itself. So they fitted the most effective forms to the space they had to fill. If the design did not turn out perfectly, they would simply add another flower or scroll and thus finish it off.

In 1970 the Norwegian-American Museum of Decorah, Iowa, sponsored a trip to Norway to study rosemaling. The trip had many highlights, not the least of which was the opportunity to watch one of the finest Hallingdal rosepainting masters, Lars Sataøyen, paint before the group. Sataøyen is descended from a long line of rosemaling masters and is a cousin of Nils Ellingsgard, himself an outstanding Hallingdal painter who has taught several years at the Norwegian-American Museum's rosemaling school. Sataøyen painted two designs on large boards using "wet-on-wet" technique—the background paint to which he applied the design was wet. He worked with amazing speed, but during the course of the demonstration several drips from a scroll began to roll down the face of the painting. Everyone held his breath. No one wanted to call the drips to Sataøyen's attention. Would he carefully wipe the drips off with a rag as we Americans would do and then repaint the original stroke? No. When he saw the drips he calmly reached up and made embellishments out of them, which added to the design and took only two seconds. Thus Sataøyen carried out the old tradition of dash and originality!

The lovely art of Early American decoration, which included painting and stenciling and was so popular in America from the end of the 1700's to the mid-1800's, is now regulated by a society, and no artist is allowed to create an original design but all must rely on reproducing existing designs. This policy has kept this particular art form from developing creatively in the last hundred years. Such a policy is directly contrary to the chief aim of rosemaling, which encourages each student as he becomes proficient enough with mixing color and brush strokes to branch out into designs of his own, using the flower and scroll forms he has learned as guidelines.

CREATING ORIGINAL DESIGNS

LEARN THE BASICS FIRST

The first thing to learn is to walk before you run. To do this, study the work of some of the old rosemalers carefully. Often it looks interesting and disarmingly simple. Again it may be complicated and full of intricate outlining. But at all times the painting looks as if the artists knew exactly what they could handle in the way of design, color, and details. Nowadays we often try things too difficult for our skills, and as a result our designs and strokes may not be successful. We all want to do elaborate designs and outlining before we can handle them. It is better to see a design painted with good brush strokes than a more involved design painted with strokes the student has not yet mastered. Therefore, *it is important to achieve control of the brush first.* No designing should be attempted until the student has a high degree of skill in this respect.

Remember that you must start with the basic principles and that the end result of learning to use the strokes perfectly is the ability and confidence to paint freely and develop your own style.

TRACING DESIGNS

The most approved and creative way of putting a design on a practice board is to sketch it on with the brush. The fluidity of the brush is frequently the only way to capture the movement of line and form in rosepainting, especially in Telemark painting. However, most rosemaling teachers start their students off by having them trace designs onto their boards with either lithopone (chalk) or charcoal. The chalk or charcoal is rubbed on the back of the piece of paper the design is on. Place the paper rubbed-side-down on the board and tape it in place, making sure it is centered correctly. Now trace over the design with a pen or pencil and the design will be transferred clearly to the board. Remember that if you either draw or trace a design using chalk or charcoal any excess marks other than the design itself should be wiped off before starting to paint. Once the design has been transferred, the student can begin to paint it; he will not have the worry of drawing the design itself until the

Figure 114. Sketching a design with a flat brush. Copyright: Margaret M. Miller

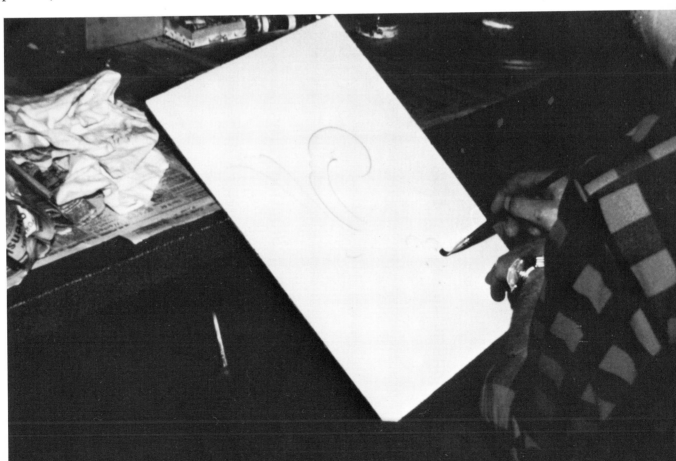

preliminary brush strokes and basic color mixing have been grasped. It cannot be emphasized too strongly at this point that *no student should trace designs for more than two or three lessons.* This can become a fatal habit that will prevent the student from ever advancing to the creative level in rosemaling. If used too long, tracing cannot fail to become a crutch that will discourage the insecure student from developing.

Perhaps the most important function of tracing is that it is a quick way for the student to build up his collection of designs. Every rosemaler needs the resource of good designs from which to draw ideas, and he also needs to get a variety of designs for his own students to use the day he becomes good enough to teach. Also, tracing designs teaches the beginner the forms of rosemaling. After tracing certain flower, scroll, leaf, and outlining forms repeatedly, the student will retain many of them in his memory to be called forth when he needs ideas for a design.

COPYING OR SKETCHING DESIGNS

After several classes students should begin to copy designs by sketching. This can be done by using an instrument such as a brush, as is commonly done in Telemark technique, or a piece of chalk or charcoal, as is most often done in Hallingdal. While this may seem frustrating at first to someone who has never sketched before, it will not be long before practice will enable you to work fairly quickly and quite accurately.

Start by deciding whether you want to oil your board before painting or if you prefer it dry. If you decide to use wet-on-wet, the first step is to rub the surface with your oil and turpentine combination. If your practice board has been rubbed with oil and turpentine first, you will *have* to sketch the design on the surface with paint and a brush. A #2 or #3 outlining brush works well, but any flat or round brush can be used for sketching. Any design previously put on the board with carbon, chalk, or charcoal will be rubbed off when you apply linseed oil and turpentine.

There are many advantages to using a wet board. One is that it encourages greater stroking smoothness; it also allows greater freedom to be original. Any part of a design that appears incorrect can easily be removed with just a wipe of your rag or your finger. The opportunity to correct a design quickly also makes it simple to balance it by either subtraction or addition.

Most symmetrical designs are drawn on a dry board. If you want to rub a little oil onto the background, you must draw the design over again with a hard pencil. Go right over the chalk or charcoal marks. The pencil mark will still show if you then rub linseed oil on carefully with a rag.

The second step is to choose the paint color for sketching most suitable to the background you are painting against. For instance, with a light background a sienna would be appropriate, with raw sienna being best on white. An off-white such as a light gray or tan works well on a dark background. By using such colors you will always find yourself sketching with a color that will blend with any other color you paint on the board and that will not interfere with or change these colors. By contrast, imagine sketching with a color such as red. Such a hue would be powerful enough to change to light pink any areas you would paint white on. Or the red could conceivably change the yellow you have mixed to a more orangy color.

Begin by making a margin around the entire board so that your sketch does not trail off the edges of the board. It is usually better to leave space around any design, especially if you are an inexperienced painter. The old painters would paint right up to and over edges, but you must have a sure hand to do so. Next, for asymmetrical designs, mark the center of the board. The hub of the design, such as the beginning of a large "C" scroll, usually begins below this point. For symmetrical designs there is a special way to divide the board before painting. This will be discussed in the next section.

Begin the actual sketching by propping up the design you are copying in front of you and drawing its central part first, whether it be a large flower, a "C" scroll, or a geometric shape. This will be the hub from which all the other forms will come and when properly placed will be a good start for the rest of the design. Try to draw carefully and get your design as close as possible to the one you are following. When sketching a design, put in only the outlines of the various scrolls, flowers, and larger leaves. Leave outlining and detail strokes to be added later without preliminary sketching. Especially do not bother to put in details *inside* of scrolls and flowers, as they will only be lost anyway when the basic design is painted.

For a beginner it is important to take one problem at a time. After sketching, mix all your colors at one time and make sure you have enough of them. Put a bit of each color on the background to see if all the hues you have mixed blend well with each other and suit the background. Now paint the colors on the design and try to balance them so the design is evenly distributed throughout as far as warmth and coolness, value, intensity, and hue are concerned.

When you begin to copy, choose a design that is simple enough for you to handle. At first try to follow the design you look at carefully. In time you will find that you have gained the ability to use the ideas in the design freely and to combine elements of other designs you remember with the one you are following. In that way, if something can be improved on or made different, you can change it for the better— the beginning of originality in design. At first you will just change the position of one scroll or add one flower, but when you change a design enough to alter its character you can say that you are creating. Then

one wonderful day you will discover that you have painted an entire design of your own. After that you will have become a true rosemaler and will never want to copy again.

LAYING OUT SYMMETRICAL AND ROUND DESIGNS

A symmetrical design poses a great challenge because it is relatively difficult for a beginner to get both sides of a design even. However, if the practice board is carefully marked into sections this obstacle can easily be hurdled. But it would be wise to refrain from tackling symmetrical designs until you are adept at sketching asymmetrical ones.

When it comes to sketching a symmetrical design it is important to mark your board off into sections. This can be done either with a ruler and chalk (or charcoal) or a string and chalk. The idea is to divide the board down the center lengthwise and then divide it one more time on each side of the center line. If the panel is a big one, you may want to divide it into even smaller areas. Now make the same marks across the width of the board so that the entire board will be composed of squares. Once these preliminary marks have been made you will have the basis for determining within what areas certain parts of the design you are sketching will go.

The work of dividing the board can be quickly done with a piece of string and chalk. Run the chalk across the string so that the string absorbs the chalk dust. Then divide the board into sections by holding the string tightly on either side of the board and having a second person snap the string so as to leave a line of chalk dust down the center of the board. Continue until the board is divided into the appropriate number of sections. How many lines you use also depends on how good a rosemaler you are. If you are a skilled artist, you may need only the middle line and one cross line to create symmetrical designs, but a beginner needs many more. If no one is available to snap the string for you, simply draw the chalk lines on with a ruler.

Once these lines are drawn begin sketching the design with chalk, working from the central part and building up. Be careful to avoid letting the design become topheavy, as symmetrical designs have a tendency to be. Symmetrical designs should be strongest in the center or toward the bottom, so they will not give a feeling of weakness. As you build up the design, make a mark on each side to get the larger scrolls even. This does not mean that the design should be *exactly* the same on both sides—just enough so that the balance is there. It is also helpful to measure the distance from the middle to the outer sides with a brush handle so that the width of each side is accurate.

It would be wise to draw the left side of the pattern first. Otherwise you will be covering up what you have done on the right side with

Figure 115. Dividing practice boards into sections is especially important in Hallingdal rosemaling. Notice how the height of each major curve has been marked in. This, as well as the dividing lines, is usually done with chalk.

your hand and arm and you won't be able to see one side of the design to compare it with the other. After the central part is drawn, continue by adding the largest scrolls and lastly work on the smaller, peripheral segments of the design. By working with chalk it is possible to wipe off a part if you change your mind.

If an object with a symmetrical design needs a border, it should be free and flowing for contrast with the balanced center design. Conversely, a symmetrical border is sometimes effective if you have an asymmetrical design.

In symmetrical and round designs you will probably pick out simpler flower forms and details than in asymmetrical ones and will use the type of tulip and petal flowers that make a natural termination rather than lead into more design.

Round designs are a challenge to paint, partly because there is no end to their possible variety. A compass is a helpful instrument in working on these designs. It will help you set up different segments, much as the string and chalk help to lay out a balanced symmetrical design.

STORY TELLING DESIGNS

We are all children of our time. As such we love to see the traditions and beliefs of our age recorded in some manner. The picture story designs satisfied this need of the Norwegians during the rosemaling years. However, it should be mentioned that this type of decoration was much more prevalent in Sweden during the same age and is more justly associated with the Swedish *blomstermåling*. Still, the Norwegians did enough picture story designs to make them worth mentioning.

The picture story designs expressed the interests of the people. Some of the most popular subjects were music, the Bible, special events, and the comings and goings of important personages in highly ornamental uniforms. Norwegian rural figures were usually dressed more informally and are pictured as fiddling, arguing, drinking, or being married.

In those days artists were not influenced by the realism that has overtaken contemporary artists because of the knowledge of perspective and the invention of the camera. Instead, they wanted only to tell a story, and they did it with primitive simplicity and enthusiasm. The brush strokes used to delineate a lady's head could be the same ones used to paint a flower. Everything—buildings, people, trees, carriages, and animals—was painted flat, with no perspective and little shading or depth. These were extremely honest and consequently historically interesting pieces of decoration. The old fiddler heartily stamping his foot in tune to his music may seem somewhat distorted to us, but he represented a joyful part of Norwegian rural life.

Figure 116. This wall painting from eastern Norway has a distinctly Swedish flavor. It is from Synvisstua at Glomdal museum. In it the son is asking his father what he can look forward to in life. The father is replying that life is like a dream and at the end is death. Copyright: De Sandvigske Samlinger

Figure 117. Quaint and important looking figures march across a small box from Ottadalen. Copyright: De Sandvigske Samlinger

LETTERING AND OLD SAYINGS

Language has been coupled with rosemaling ever since this form of decoration began. It was of great importance for the dowry chest to be inscribed with the initials of the bride and the bride's father, or with their full names. Besides names, dates, and initials, items were often decorated with sayings that could be humorous, lyrical, or crude, reflecting the wisdom of rural Norway and the morals and habits of a family. Favorite bits of poetry, prose, or religious quotations were popular, and were of great pride to the family since they reflected their strivings toward a certain life-style. In spite of the use of popular sayings, *the basic Norwegian tradition is that of informal original sayings lettered in good Norwegian.* Sometimes the saying was made up on the spur of the moment; or it might have been a favorite family expression that had been treasured through the years. This tradition should be followed nowadays; use your own imagination or memories about the family to give the saying special meaning to those who see it. Sayings that are appropriate to a time, place, or particular item are good, too. Again, it should be stressed that the Norwegian tradition is for sayings to be original rather than stereotyped or frequently repeated.

The following sayings represent only a few that illustrate the previous points about suitability and originality.

On a shoehorn is painted the saying: "Den vet hvor skoen trykker som har den på," or, "The one who wears the shoe knows where it hurts."

Figure 118. Dowry chest. Copyright: De Sandvigske Samlinger

*Figure 119. Typical West Coast painting from 1834. Done in Nord-Møre.
Notice the beautiful lettering. Copyright: Norsk Folkemuseum (Oslo)*

On beer bowls in particular it was common to paint sayings that reflected the use of the article. Such quotations usually admonished the drinker to beware the power of liquor. A Valdres beer bowl contains a unique invitation to guests:

> Heil og sael; gjer vel og sit.
> Drikk av meg, men drikk med vit.

Freely translated, this saying means, "Greetings and happiness; come in and sit. Drink with me, but drink with sense." Of course, such a saying is quite poetic in Norwegian and loses some of its charm in translation.

An old painter once got away with lettering on a cabinet, "The housewife wanted this cabinet painted because she is too lazy to clean it."

Inside a bowl a twelve-year-old child rosemaled the following: "Den største gleda ein kan ha, det er å gjera andre glad." "The greatest pleasure one can have is to make others happy."

A man who wanted to keep cars off his property had a gate built and on it was lettered this bit of poetry:

> Velkomen på fotom gåand,
> Men lat bilen bi ute ståand.

Loosely translated, it means, "Welcome walking on your feet, and leave the car out in the street."

Figure 120. Early bowl with printed lettering. Copyright: De Sandvigske Samlinger

Around the inside rim of a bowl was lettered, "Vil du eta med lyst, ma du streva fyrst." "If you want to eat with pleasure, you have to work hard first."

Another bowl poetically describes the new life a tree has been given: "Av gamalt tre fra Noregs jord, der fugler på kvisten kveda, eg forma vart til fat pa bord i heimen tel hugnad og gleda." "Of old wood from Norway's earth where birds sing on the branch, I was shaped into a dish on the table in the home for happiness and joy."

In present-day rosemaling, the use of lettering is often an Americanism and sayings are sometimes a mixture of Swedish and Norwegian. Traditionally, lettering was not used around plates but rather on the outside of bowls and beer tankards, and it never detracted from the design itself. Today, however, it is quite common to letter the edges of plates, and most contemporary rosemalers feel that even though it is not traditional, if it is important to the person who owns the plate to have lettering, it is right to use it. If you wish to do so, place the lettering around the rim or on half of the rim, leaving the remainder free for a design. Initials can be placed in the center of the plate with the design circling them, but in all cases the lettering should not interfere with the design itself.

Lettering was frequently of high quality in Norway. Each rosemaler had his own style of calligraphy, and this lettering became a part of the design while never overpowering it. When lettering was used on an old cabinet or chest, it was so well keyed to the rest of the design it would be the last thing noticed.

The fine old lettering came from the brushes they used. This lettering is hard to duplicate because our brushes today are different; still, with practice your lettering should be very close to the old style.

It is considered better if the lettering is done in a style to match the painting. While fine lettering was common all around the country, much of the finest came from Valdres, where the lettering was done in perfect taste and in a simpler style to match the more basic designs common to Valdres painting. In Hallingdal the lettering was thicker and bolder to match the painting, whereas in Telemark, a more delicate, flowing script was used because it was so appropriate to the Telemark style of graceful, fluid lines.

Paint your own lettering in colors that are already a part of the rosemaling design rather than stark black and white or any color that will not blend well with the design itself. Try to put the lettering near the top or on the edge of a piece so that it does not command the center of a design. Initials and dates may be incorporated into the centers of designs, but names and sayings should be reserved for border areas.

Figure 121. A beautiful chest from Valdres. The black background is typical of that area. Some of the finest lettering was done in Valdres. Copyright: Norsk Folkemuseum (Oslo)

A B C D E F

M N O P R

a b c d e f g h i j k l m

A C D E O

Marit G derf

Norwegian Script Lettering

Artist: S. Aarseth

GKIJKL

TUVWY

nopprsTUvy1972

Mav Tore N II

r god SKI

7
Advanced Rosemaling Techniques and Concepts

THE IDEAS PUT FORTH in this chapter range from general concepts and more abstract attitudes about rosemaling to advanced techniques that can be described in specific terms. Both areas, however, are in the realm that has special interest for the mature rosemaling painter. These are the areas that require a high degree of creative originality and a background of several years of intensive experience. They also require a skill with mixing colors and with brushwork that has become so sound as to be second nature.

ADVANCED BRUSH TECHNIQUE

PAINTING IN DIFFERENT DIRECTIONS

Chapter 5 stated a rule that does not necessarily apply to advanced rosepainters: in flat brush technique the beginner should start flowers and scrolls on the outside edge. This does not hold true for the expert who is skilled in brush handling technique. Such a person can derive many interesting effects from bringing outside strokes over inside ones. Not only does this kind of variation in brushwork lend dash and charm to a design, it shows off the painter's skill as well. (See Figure 122.)

TWO-TONE TECHNIQUE

Two-tone brush technique is the ability to paint two colors at one time using one brush. This technique is not difficult to acquire, but the effective choice of colors and the perfection of its use are difficult and best left to the mature painter.

The outstanding effect achieved by this method is the subtly dramatic delineation with line and color of a leaf, a petal, or a curve. While one color is filling in the main part of the leaf, the other color is putting an edge on it that lends contrast. The edge also acts as outlining, so

154

Figure 122. This panel effectively illustrates graceful movement of line as well as follow-through of line. It is also an excellent example of strong value contrast and shows how outside strokes can be brought over inside strokes, especially on curves. Copyright: Kolbein Dahle

Figure 123. This plate, by artist Gunnar Nordbø, is an exellent illustration of two-tone technique. It also provides fine examples of the use of broken lines in outlining, the follow-through of lines, and the use of details and lines to help support heavy flowers. Crosshatching, which was not too common in Telemark, is cleverly added to give weight to stems. Copyright: T. Johansen

two steps are accomplished at one time. Flat brushes of any size are the most effective for this technique, which also imparts dimension, since the use of a lighter and darker color create the appearance of light and shadow.

To try out this type of painting, load your brush with the main color. Wipe this color off the corner of the brush and then lay it carefully on its side edge in the second color. If you are at all careless in dipping the brush into the second color, you will lose the clear-cut separation of colors which is so important. The second color should extend as close to the ferrule of the brush as possible in order to carry any great distance along a stroke. Usually the second color will not carry the entire length of a long scroll. In such a case, and contrary to technique, the stroke should be broken and continued at the point of break. A finishing stroke should then be taken inside these strokes to cover the break.

The brush should be completely cleaned after only a few strokes when using two colors. Otherwise they will begin to blend together on the brush. This would nullify the two-color effect of the stroke and might even cause muddying.

It is possible to use three colors on one brush but you would only be able to paint small areas such as leaf forms. Filling a leaf with one stroke using green and mustard for the main part and black for the edge is only one of many effective combinations. To do this properly, your brush probably should be at least a #5.

You may ask, "Why use two-tone technique in some areas instead of simply outlining?" The reason is because colors put on in this way have a special clarity and sharpness, as well as a unified flow that shows they were made at the same time with one stroke of the brush. This effect is very beautiful.

Round brushes can also be used for two-tone effects but in quite a different way. Begin by working one color into the hairs of the brush. Then dip into another color with the tip of the brush. Simply by using the brush in the usual way you can create a two-tone teardrop. Many of the flower petals in Hallingdal style are painted in this way.

You can also use three colors in a round brush. For example, fill the brush with yellow and then clean most of it out so that some is left close to the ferrule. Dip the rest of the brush in white and then dip the point in blue. Make a teardrop with firm pressure so that the yellow comes out at the end of the stroke.

This technique of using several colors on one brush should be employed with great discrimination. Select the flowers and scrolls where this effect will be most important and confine it to those areas. As with outlining, two-tone painting can be overdone and is most effective when well but discreetly used.

There are several other techniques for achieving the sculptured, dimensional effect of two-tone painting. Try these with scroll strokes first, as the result can best be seen with large strokes.

One is to lay down the most intense, or darkest, color first. Wait a few minutes and repaint over the scroll, retracing the exact area previously painted except this time using a lighter color. Waiting before repainting is important as it prevents complete absorption of the light color by the darker one.

Again, paint a scroll with one color. Now wipe the brush off on newspaper and apply the dry brush to the inside area of the scroll, taking up color onto the brush as it passes over the painted area. This will lighten the inside edge and give a lovely two-tone effect with two shades of one color. In this case it is not necessary to wait a few minutes for the paint to set.

OUTLINING THE DRY BOARD

In the 1800's some Hallingdal artists put a great deal of stress on pronounced outlining. To get this effect they often let the design dry before outlining it.

If you decide to try this technique you must be sure to add at least ¼ turpentine to the colors mixed for the basic design. If you use only oil, the paint will be too slick and the outlining will skip off the design as it passes over it. The outcome will cause extreme frustration and a bad result. It takes a rather experienced hand to add the turpentine because too much of it will cause the paint to run.

Turpentine will also help you out if you should inadvertently let your board dry. Wipe over the design with turpentine first, rubbing vigorously, and the outlining will often stick. Another help for the accidentally dry board is to blow your breath on an area of the board and quickly outline while the moisture is condensed in that spot.

ADVANCED OUTLINING OF LEAVES AND FLOWERS

With leaf forms it is extremely important to have good variations in the length of the outlining strokes. Leaves can develop a sameness, but line variety shows movement and life. Here you will notice that the outlining often takes the form of waves, rising and falling with the length of the strokes. With this idea should be stressed the additional concept that if you develop a more complicated leaf form out of a basic stroke, such as a "C" or an "S," you should still be able to see this simple form through it.

There are generally three reasons for a flower: to fill a space, to show a movement, and to stop a movement. Often it is the space left for a flower form that determines the size or shape of the flower, not that a designated space is left for a certain flower to fill up. Flowers should indicate movement by the flow of action up their stems and through the details coming out of their tops. They can stop action by being placed at the borders of a design or by their lack of continuation, with no details coming out their tops. They should never grow from long stems, suspended out in space by themselves where they will tend to let the design fly apart.

Figure 124. The form of the "S" curve, upon which this design is based, can be clearly seen through the intricate detail surrounding it. Copyright: Kolbein Dahle

Figure 125. Using the liner brush and stick. Copyright: Margaret M. Miller

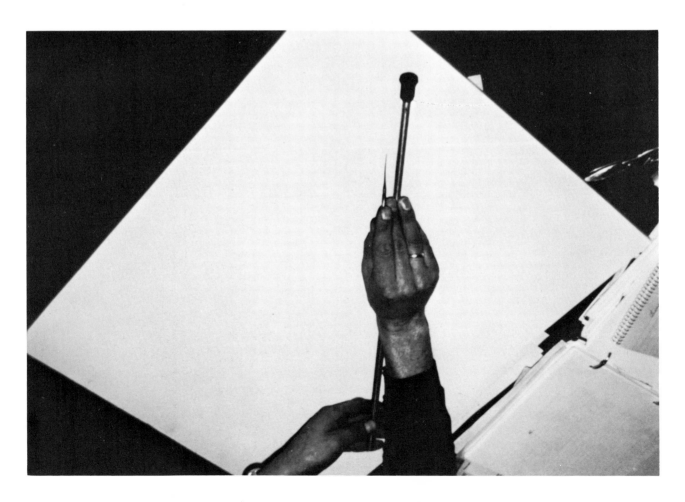

USING THE LINER BRUSH AND STICK

To draw a straight, thin line around the edge of a board or object, hold the liner brush between the thumb and first and second fingers. Run the third and fourth fingers along the edge of the board, carrying the brush along to produce the line. It has been found to be easier to use a liner brush without a handle for this technique. To draw a line anywhere on the inside of the board, use the liner stick. Rest the end of the stick on the hand not holding the brush and run the hand which is holding the brush along the stick. The liner stick is also useful for supporting your painting hand when long thin outlining strokes are needed on a design.

If your hand should be damp from perspiration it will jerk along, causing an uneven line. Rub chalk on your fingers and your hand will again run smoothly along.

Figure 126. If you want to use the liner brush to line near the edge of an object, the second and third fingers are used as guides to direct the hand along the edge of the object. Copyright: Margaret M. Miller

Figure 127. Cabinet owned and painted by S. Aarseth. The panels of this piece are done in very transparent colors, as can be clearly seen in the detail photo, and are somewhat similar to old rosepainting in the valley of Ø. Slidre. The top of the cabinet has been treated with lasur graining. Copyright: Kolbein Dahle

TRANSPARENT TECHNIQUE

The rosemaling technique called "transparent" has been previously mentioned; it employs colors so thin that the background can be seen through the design painting. This style is especially attractive when the design is limited to one or two colors. It then achieves a delicate, almost ethereal look that is seldom found in other rosemaling. Actually very few contemporary rosemalers know how to use this technique and it should be revived.

The Sense of Space or "Air"

Transparency gives a feeling of space or "airiness" to a design. Some types of rosemaling do not need this. For example, in Hallingdal the painting technique itself is strong and opaque. There is a firmness in

the size of the lines, in the thickness or opacity of the color, and in the shape of the design. The need to have a sense of "air" was here solved by using simpler, more open designs. In Telemark, where the painters tend to fill up almost all space, this airy feeling comes from combining the opaque colors with the transparent colors that give a sense of air and delicacy. A thin, transparent crimson, for instance, on a red background, creates this light, airy effect.

The Effect of Transparent Technique on Color

The effect of the background color on transparent rosemaling color is especially evident when the background color is strong. For example, if you have decided to use red for your background color and then choose to cover it with a vivid Prussian blue (which has considerable green) in a transparent type of painting, you will find that it will look almost gray when painted on top of the red even if you take the color directly from the tube. The red background color showing through kills the green (its complement) and takes it out of the blue. Similar changes in color resulting from transparency are noticeable to a certain degree with every color, since the background color showing through changes any color painted on it. This is one reason why this technique is so different and why a complete understanding of color composition is necessary to handle it effectively. This is especially true when opacity and transparency are combined and a great many colors are used. The situation is eased somewhat when a design is painted with *only* transparent colors, usually either monochromatic or using one or two colors alone. Then a great knowledge of color is not necessary.

When transparent color was used in old rosemaling it was often painted on quite casually and later, as it faded out, the outlining brought out the design. Where the design itself was most casual the painters would paint the outlining outside the design elements, thus showing background color between the design color and the outlining. This made the design more interesting. If the colors were dark and the forms pronounced, the outlining had to follow the forms and was usually thicker and more dominant.

Painting Transparent Technique

The idea behind transparent painting is to eventually shade the colors out completely. This means you must use the paint so thinly you can hardly see it.

Start by oiling the surface to be painted. Then mix the usual combination of linseed oil and add a few drops of varnish. In transparent painting it is very evident if you are using too much or too little varnish, because with too much varnish the brush will stick and with too little the thin paint will run. Practicing with this technique is an excellent way to learn how much varnish makes a good consistency of paint. Next

Figure 128. Base strokes in transparent painting. In the first photo the brush is still painting even though the color is nearly gone. There is a distinct contrast in the values in this technique. Copyright: Kolbein Dahle

Figure 129. Outlining transparent technique on next pages. Copyright: Kolbein Dahle

add the color and dip your brush into it, using less paint and oil on the brush hairs than you would normally. Then wipe the brush off on newspaper to rid it of any excess before starting to paint. The paint color will begin by being close to normal but gradually will become thinner and thinner with each successive stroke until there is almost no paint left in the brush and the background shows through clearly. In transparent painting the brush should be replenished as seldom as possible.

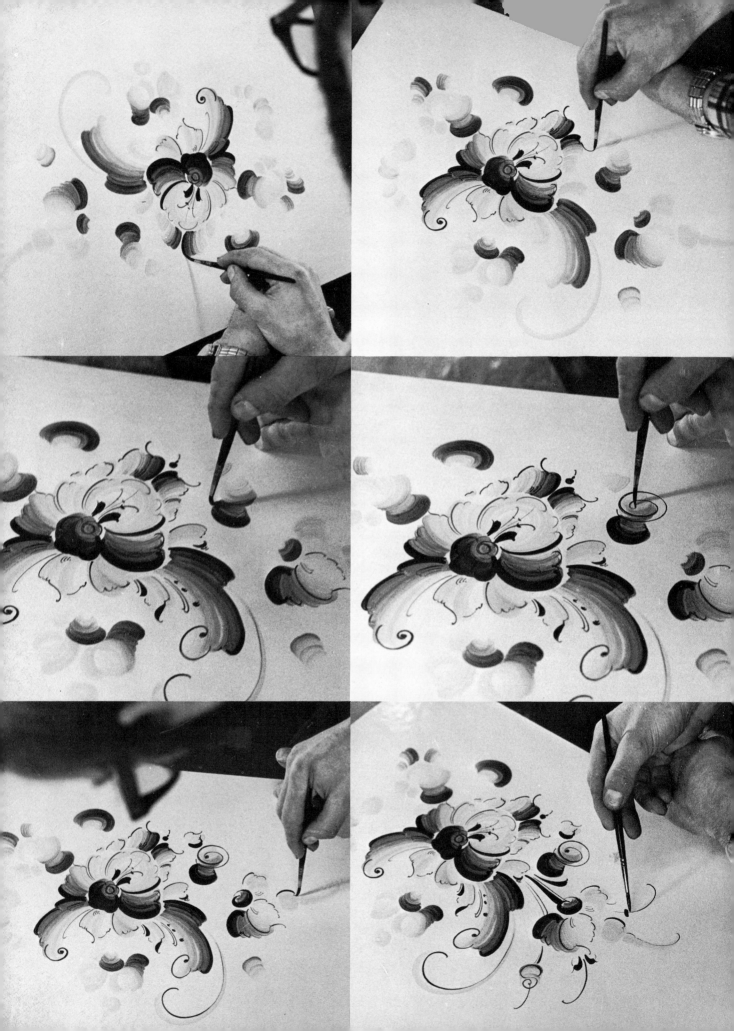

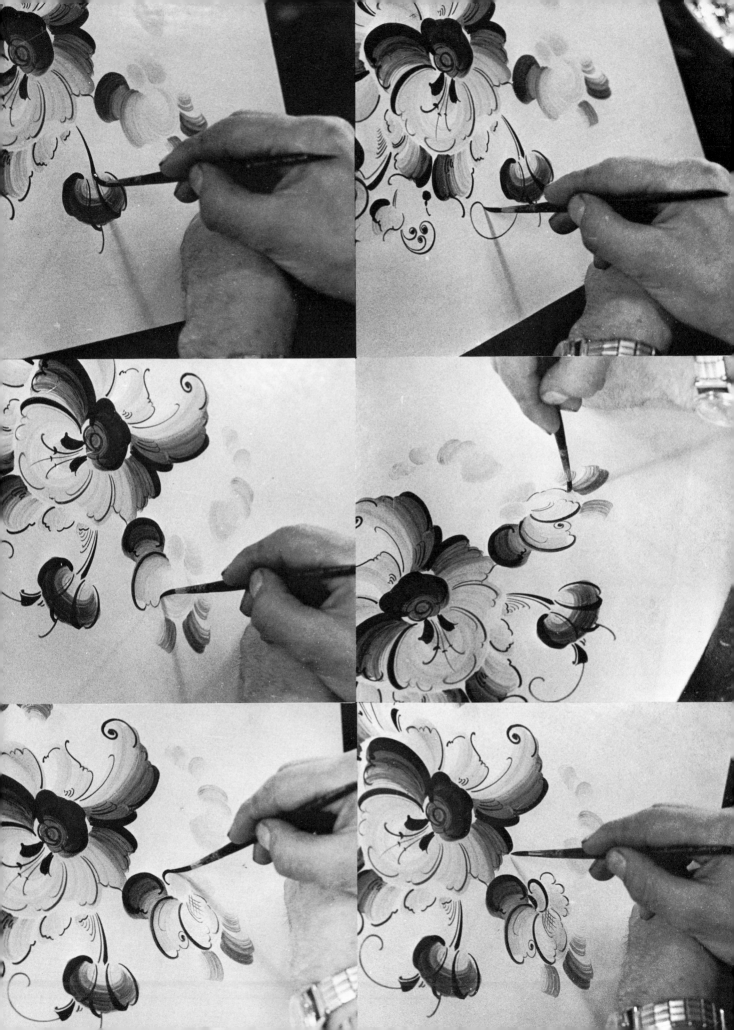

Figure 130. Notice how strong the outlining becomes when used over curves which have been transparently painted. This illustrates why outlining should be discreetly used when painting with transparent technique.

When painting with a transparent technique, the colors can be much closer to the pure hue than ordinarily. The reason for this is that the background tends to act as a toner since it shows through the paint.

Outlining Transparent Technique

As mentioned before, outlining usually received more emphasis in transparent painting than standard rosemaling, for it is the outlining rather than the basic painting that brings out the design. Still one must be careful, because outlining, if too heavy or lacking in variety, can become so dominant as to kill this subtle type of design. Outlining usually follows the line of design, but it can add more interest if placed a little outside of the design. Do not overdo this, though. Instead, try to add variety to your style of outlining, with some strokes outside but most of them close to the design. Try to keep your basic painting strokes free; if they are too exact there is little need for outlining and the effect becomes stiff and commercial.

GOLD LEAFING

Gold leaf was mainly used in the Telemark district to add richness to elaborate designs. The old rosemalers liked to use gold leaf for the center of flowers and then put a transparent glaze over the entire design.

It is important to appreciate the strength of gold leaf and to use it with restraint—as an accent only! Using too much cheapens it. Antiquing over gold leaf will tend to muddy it unless a transparent color such as green umber or green earth is used. These colors will allow the gold leaf to shine through the paint and retain its genuine look. There must be some glaze over the gold or it will stand out too prominently and dominate the design. If you do not use genuine gold leaf you will have to cover it with a glaze to prevent it from oxidizing.

Materials for Gold Leafing

Genuine gold leaf is twenty-three carat gold and can be purchased, as can the other supplies for gold leafing, from any good art supply store. When genuine, it is labeled "XX deep" and comes in small, square packages of twenty-five sheets called leaves. Each leaf is carefully packed between two sheets of paper. The characteristic color of real gold leaf is a deep, rich gold; it has a slightly bluish-green cast when held to the light. This color differentiates it from imitation, or "Dutch," gold, which is more gray in tone.

The special brush used to apply gold leaf is known as a "Gilder's Tip." It is a peculiar brush 4½″ wide with hairs 2¼″ long, and it is made of camel's hair.

The varnish which is used as the adhesive and painted on the areas to be gold-leafed is usually marked "quick" or "slow." "Hutchins Gold" is a standard brand of this varnish. The quick varnish is ready to take the leaf in one to three hours, depending on atmospheric conditions. However, it can be slowed down by the addition of oil colors. Slow varnish dries in twenty to twenty-four hours and is preferred by most gold leafers if the job is a big one. The choice between quick or slow varnish depends usually on whether you will be able to finish gold leafing the same day or will need to allow time for it the next day.

How to Apply Gold Leaf

Gold leaf works best when put onto a semi-gloss surface such as is normally used for rosemaling. Paint the area to be treated with gold with the special varnish. If you wish, you can add a little color, such as yellow ochre, to the varnish so that you can see the area to be gilded more easily. However, use very, very little color. Wait the required time to apply gold leaf but to be doubly sure, keep checking the varnish. When it feels basically dry but still a little sticky it is ready for the leaf. If it is not dry enough the gold will "drown," or disappear, but if it is too dry the gold will not stick. It is wise to paint a small sample board first to see if the sticky quality is right. Do not remove the gold leaf from its protective paper before cutting out the size piece you need. Take your Glider's Tip and work electricity from your hair into the brush by rubbing it back and forth briskly on your head. Now remove the covering layer of paper from the side over the gold and slowly pick it up.

The electricity will cause the leaf to stick to the brush. Lay the gold on to the sticky area and carefully stroke it with the brush. The gold can now be rubbed in with a firmer brush or a cotton ball. If you rub a hole in the gold, pick up a small piece of leaf with your fingers and lay it over the hole. If you are planning to antique on top of genuine gold you must varnish it first, for it is so thin it may not hold up.

FINISHING TECHNIQUES

VARNISHING

The simplest way to protect and preserve rosemaling is to varnish the dry design with one or two coats of a low-gloss or satin varnish. Some people will choose a shiny varnish and some a dull. However, it is well to realize that too dull a finish will kill the brilliancy of the colors and too high-gloss a finish is not characteristic of rosemaling. Some people prefer to apply many coats of varnish with gentle sanding in between to give the smooth, satiny finish that some rosemalers prefer, but which is not recommended as it is more typical of decoupage than rosemaling.

The most durable varnish is of the high-gloss type. If you use this varnish, be sure to reduce the gloss by using pumice between each coat. However, this makes a great deal of work and if the object you have rosemaled has a good finish, one thin coat of a satin varnish should suffice to protect it. Most rosemalers feel it is best to use as little varnish as possible to keep a piece looking more natural. Before you apply the varnish be sure to wipe off all traces of finger marks, oil, chalk, and pencil. If you have trouble removing these marks it is possible to wipe them off with a little turpentine without harming the paint, because oil paint, when dried, should be quite impervious to turpentine.

ANTIQUING

Antiquing is a favorite finishing technique of rosemalers, and justly so. It gives an authentically old look to the work because it softens and dulls the colors.

Antiquing can be done by one of three methods: (1) antiquing the painted board, letting it dry, and then painting the design on the board; (2) antiquing over the board and design after the design has been painted on and dried (the most popular method); and (3) antiquing both before and after the design is painted. This will cause the board background to recede more and allow the design to stand out, but not as markedly as in (1).

Recipe for Antiquing Mixture
It is difficult to give an exact recipe for an antiquing mixture because it will depend on how heavy you want the antiquing and how large the project is that you intend to antique. For best results and an authentically old look, use the old-fashioned materials, a mixture of oil and turpentine. The usual proportions are about three parts oil to one part turpentine. With smaller objects a few drops of varnish may be added to the mixture to speed the drying. If the object is large, leave the varnish out, as it will cause the mixture to become sticky and dry too fast. Nowadays the oil is of such good quality that it can be used pure as an antiquing medium without anything being added to it.

Stirring the Antiquing Mixture
Basic to good antiquing is a knowledge of how to stir the antiquing mixture so it is completely blended. Begin your mixture by pouring out enough oil to cover the bottom of a jar or can. Next add the powder or tube color to the oil. Stir thoroughly until well mixed. When these are blended, continue to thin the mixture to the proper consistency by adding the mixture of oil and turpentine gradually. If you were to add the color directly to a large amount of solution you would not be able to blend the color in completely.

Keep adding and mixing the color to the solution of turpentine and oil until you reach the desired shade, using a touch of black or one of the umbers for the darker finishes.

Unlike your own antiquing mixture, which is easy to work with, the antiquing kits sold on the market are hard to work with and will allow you no control over the color.

Selecting Antiquing Colors
In making the antiquing mixture, you have a choice of the antiquing color you will use, but it is important to choose transparent rather than opaque colors. If you simply want to give an old mellow look, use raw or burnt umber, the two preferred antiquing colors.

On a light background such as an off-white you can use nearly any transparent color for antiquing, whereas on a medium to dark background it is best to use a color that is closely allied to the background color. For instance, on a fairly vibrant red background you can use a burnt umber, but on a softer, duller red a burnt sienna would be a better choice.

Applying Antiquing Mixture
When the antiquing mixture is ready, brush the stain onto the area you wish to cover. Let it stand for a few minutes and then wipe it off to the desired shade with a clean rag. Another way to handle the finishing of an object is to use the palm of your hand instead of a rag for the final

rubbing. Use a circular motion to work the color into the paint ridges. This technique is especially effective when using the thicker paint of Hallingdal style, since the antiquing will catch in the ridges of the paint and leave interesting darker areas.

If you are antiquing a piece of furniture with moldings or edgings of one kind or another, it is effective to leave the antiquing slightly darker in the corners. It gives the piece an older look when the stain is a little uneven.

A wonderful Norwegian antiquing finish is made by using green umber from the tube with oil and turpentine and a few drops of varnish for fast drying. This color is similar to burnt umber but gives an aged, more greenish tinge to objects on which it is used.

Other Methods of Antiquing

If an even older effect is desired it can be achieved in several ways. The first is by sanding your design with the finest grade of carborundum paper, known as "waterproof silicone carbide" before doing the antiquing. Sand enough so that some of the design is rubbed away in spots.

A second method is to use a blow torch; it will give the very ancient "burnt up" look that is normally produced only by the heat and wear of many years. This blow torch burning can be done to the background first and the process can be repeated after the design has been painted on. After the burning, rub the object with a wire brush. Next rub on thinned black oil paint and then wipe it off. If you desire an even older look, sand down both the background and the design with a fine sandpaper.

Figure 131. Rosemaling on beams with lasur treatment on the ceiling. Painting by Sigmund Aarseth. Copyright: Kolbein Dahle

LASUR TECHNIQUE

"Lasur" is the Norwegian word for "glaze." This term appears to have originated from the Persian word for lapis lazuli, *lazward*, which became corrupted in Italian to *l'azzure*, in French to *l'azure*, the name of the stone coming to represent its color, a deep shade of blue. During the period of Louis XV the fashion was prevalent in France to finish furniture with a tinted varnish, or glaze and in particular the French often used an azure blue for their glaze.

The difference between antiquing and lasuring is that antiquing tries to subdue the colors of the decorating to give it an old look, while lasur does the reverse. It picks up the brilliancy of the color and makes no attempt to make it look old. Whereas antiquing tones down colors, lasur often brightens them. Antiquing is usually done on top of the decoration; lasur is generally a transparent color used on top of the background color only and is calculated to assist that color by modifying it. The following are a few principles of lasur which will be of assistance to the artist:

A lasur color that is analogous to the ground will result in a softly changed and deepened tone.

A lasur finish that is a complement of the ground, such as red over green, will result in a neutralized hue.

A glaze that is deeper in value than the ground increases the warmth of the surface.

A warm colored lasur glaze over a darker warm tone usually produces a cool, silvery effect.

A light neutral glaze over a dark color gives a warm intensity.

These are the most common rules to remember when using lasur on a background. The color principles that apply to lasur can also apply to transparent painting.

In the olden days, lasur was used in several interesting ways. Sometimes it was simply rubbed on with an unevenness of application. Other times the glaze was applied with an old brush to simulate wood graining or marble. Most commonly the lasur glaze was used as decoration in itself to cover walls, ceilings, or beams with no decoration painted over it. When this was done the glaze was often stippled so that it had a swirled effect. This can be done easily by cutting a potato in half and twisting it in the glaze after the glaze has been applied to a surface. All over Norway rosemalers still use lasur technique. Some have been known to stipple with a cork or to turn a piece of skin or rag in the glaze. A brush is also a frequently used tool in lasuring; it can be twisted to create still another effect. During the 1970 Rosemaling Tour sponsored by the Norwegian-American Museum a well-known woodcarver in the Gulbrandsdal district was visited. This man gave a demonstration of lasuring technique. His glaze consisted of a mixture of powdered colors, powdered chalk (a substitute for varnish similar to our Spackle, which prevents running), linseed oil, stand oil, and a special fast drying oil. All this was stirred carefully and then applied with a brush to a carved cabinet, the wood of which had previously been prepared with a thin coat of varnish. The final step was to wipe the glaze lightly with a rag.

As a rule, the preparation for lasuring is not so elaborate. The lasur mixture is prepared in the same way as the antiquing mixture except that most people add a few drops of varnish to speed the drying process. Before the mixture is applied, the surface is sanded lightly. Then the colored lasur mixture is rubbed evenly onto the area to be glazed with a rag. The lasur color chosen should be a close neighbor to the background color. For example, raw sienna would be the obvious choice to vitalize and beautify a yellow. In the same way the choice of green earth would produce a lovely lasur glaze for green.

The old rosemalers did not actually strive to copy wood graining with lasur, but their surfaces remind one of it. This effect is the result of a rather difficult technique that requires a skillful hand. The simplest method is to paint the glaze on first. Then take a smaller flat brush with a darker color and let the brush roll down the board in a natural, rather jagged way. Now take a larger flat brush, which is either clean or has a little of the background color in it, and pull it through the graining line either across or down. If you decide to put a white stripe next to the darker line, do so by wiping the color off with a rag. This subject and that of using lasur for marbling will not be explored further. Both techniques are quite complex and entire books have been written on them in Norwegian.

ADVANCED CONCEPTS

PERFECTIONISM vs INDIVIDUALISM

In the chapter on brush strokes perfectionism was stressed. The beginner in any art form must strive for perfection in technique, but once he achieves it he should strive to become as individualistic as he can. If he tries to suppress this individualism his work will become commercially repetitive and he will find himself doing the same things over and over; his style will be stiff, leaving no room for experimentation and development. Understand, however, that it is one thing to paint freely and another to be careless so that you have only errors. Actually, there seem to be three stages through which the proficient rosemaler passes on the way to creative individualism: the first stage is marked by the struggle to acquire technique; the second stage is marked by the ability to make strokes perfectly and the struggle with design; and the third is the

Figure 132. Individuality and freshness in design can be seen in these designs. The panel details show great spontaneity and a restraint in the use of detail which allows the design to take precedence. The old chest, by contrast, features outlining which is dominating and actually forms the design which has been very transparently painted. Copyright: Kolbein Dahle (panels); De Sandvigske Samlinger (chest)

Figure 133. Here is a fine example of line follow-through. The forceful movement of line continues through the curves and into the outlining, especially in the carry-through of stems. Copyright: Kolbein Dahle

stage where the artist becomes so skilled in both technique and traditional design that he can be fresh and free in the variation of each through his own individuality.

Remember that rosemaling should not look like china painting. Small variations from stylized perfection are often charming and should be left in a design to give it a more handcrafted look. If some paint ridges appear, leave them alone. It is good to see occasional brush strokes and the texture. As stated before, the rosemalers in earlier days were quite brave; if part of a design did not come out as anticipated, they simply added some touches and left it. Stress was on developing a personal style, not on imitation.

Rosemaling, like any other art form, must reflect creative thinking and discrimination on the part of the painter. More than this, however, the truly fine artist feels his style inside him, and this individualism comes out in his work. To be able to use individual style and suit the design to the object in an artistic fashion is the mark of the finished rosemaler.

CONCEPTS OF DYNAMIC DESIGNING

Beginners often fall into the error of making all the flowers and leaves sprout out from a curve in just one monotonous fashion. The mature artist should try to think in terms of variety. A mixture of shorter and longer lines, of straighter and more curved lines that intertwine, of flowers and leaves in a variety of forms will create an interesting and dynamic design that has a sense of action and movement. This variety is one of the concepts that makes rosemaling typically Norwegian and harkens back to the days of the restless Viking spirit.

Movement of Line
The line of mature rosemaling should sweep out gracefully from scrolls and curves like water spurting from a fountain; it should not be stiff and static as in the more simplistic styles of other folk arts.

There are several ways to implement the concept of this free, graceful line. One is to break the movement of the line with another direction or shape, to add interest to the whole. If you have free movement in the lines and scrolls, you must have freedom in the flower and leaf forms that continue this feeling. For example, if a small, stiff flower with a set number of petals is used throughout a design, it will become monotonous and static. Instead, the effort should be toward the use of as many different forms as possible; try to stay away from the overuse of naturalistic forms, as they have a tendency to hamper the building up of a design. This is especially true if the design is large.

Figure 134. Straight lines created dynamic force. The stems in this closeup illustrate this principle. All straight lines have some minimal amount of curve. Copyright: Kolbein Dahle

It has been said that the finest artists can break the rules. This applies especially to design in rosemaling. While the curved line has been stressed throughout this book, the straight line is frequently used by expert rosemalers to add dynamic force and line movement to a design. Such a line is usually basically straight, with very slight curvature, and introduced into the design in the detail strokes and the stems of flowers.

Leaves and flowers in particular can display wide variety and from a simple form great complexity can be developed. While this variety gives life to the design, the shapes should never become so complicated that the basic form cannot be seen through them. Beware of leaves painted on top of a larger form at such an angle that they look as if they are falling off it, and of flowers that are way out on the end of a long stem. Both give the impression that they are about to fall apart and are not really a part of the overall design. Rather than creating an impression of dynamic relation, they convey the idea of suspended action.

Adapting Designs to Space

Another clue to dynamic design is the avoidance of repetition and the creative relation of a figure to the shape of the area to be decorated. While it is fine to use some round forms in round spaces and some square

Figure 135. The same base stroke, painted with transparent technique, has been outlined several different ways, pointing out the variety outlining can give one form. Copyright: Kolbein Dahle

Figure 136. The incorrect way to attach leaves to the top of a flower is shown on the left, where the leaves are too far apart and look about to fall over. The leaves on the right are closer, and because some of each leaf is implied as being under the flower it is growing from, the leaves have become part of this design element.

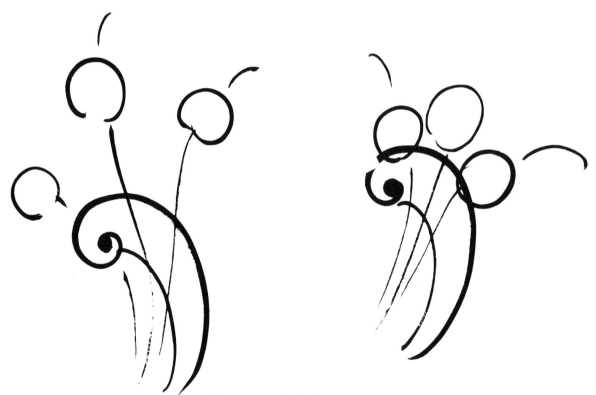

Figure 137. It is important in rosemaling to compact designs. This is to prevent various elements from flying off into space. In the example on the left the flowers tend to scatter whereas in the example on the right they are clustered close enough to the scroll to help tie the design together.

Figure 138. Unless a rose-maling design is planned to be quite simple there should not be much open space in it, especially in Telemark painting. The example on the left shows a typical open space and the example on the right illustrates how to fill such an area.

Figure 139. A simple and clear example of fitting a design to a space in an appropriate way, this mug was painted by Buskerud of Ål, Hallingdal, in 1859. Copyright: Norsk Folkemuseum (Oslo)

forms in square spaces, you might find it interesting to juxtapose unusually shaped designs. In fact, you will find that a round-shaped form in a square area sometimes fits better and is more interesting, and vice versa.

Naturalism in Design

Still another way to achieve a dynamic quality in designing is to paint the elements of the design in a natural position. For instance, leaves painted on top of a flower should seem to continue from the line of

Figure 140. Old rosepainting on a dowry chest. The suitability of the design to the spaces between the wrought-iron bands was well planned by the artist. Notice how different sized teardrops have been used to compose the design. Copyright: De Sandvigske Samlinger

growth of the stems. The stems of flowers, if carried on beyond the blossom, should be on a continuing line through the flower—even if interrupted—and not look as though they have been distorted or were an afterthought. The same is true of scrolls. They should be of continuous form; each scroll that grows out from another scroll should look as though it is a continuation of the same line of growth.

Use of Broken Lines

The skilled use of the broken or interrupted line also helps create dynamic rosemaling designs, especially in the case of outlining. Just as the human body takes on activity and life if drawn with broken lines, so leaves, flowers, and scrolls achieve great variety when broken lines of unequal length and thickness are used. If instead of outlining a long scroll with one stroke you decide to break it, you will find the scroll more interesting—as long as the breaks are planned and continue along a

Figure 141. Naturalism in design as expressed by old and new rosemaling. The door panel is from the Fossheim Hotel, Lom, and the chest was painted by S. Aarseth. In both designs the flowers follow a natural growth pattern. Copyright: De Sandvigske Samlinger (panel), Kolbein Dahle (chest)

definite line. Leaves along with scrolls particularly lend themselves to the broken line in outlining. Here the variation in the length of the line often takes the shape of waves. To break a scroll, paint along it as far as you can go, break the stroke, and continue on. Not only does breaking a stroke add interest, it gives more opportunity to add details at the point of the break and creates a sense of action by starting and stopping lines.

Figure 142. The dotted lines in these examples illustrate how stems should follow through flowers, leaves, and scrolls in a naturalistic fashion.

KEEPING ROSEMALING NORWEGIAN

The most important single thing a rosemaler can do for his art is to keep rosemaling Norwegian. What this means is to avoid letting it slip off into the areas of other folk arts so that it loses its national identity. There are several ways to ensure against this, and these are enumerated below.

Colors must retain their Norwegian quality. All colors must fall into the category of Norwegian hues. They must be muted colors that have a great strength; they are never soft and sweet, nor are they loud and garish.

Color and design must have variety. Constant uncreative copying detracts from the basic concept of rosemaling, which has always stood for originality and individuality in designing.

Rosemaling painting must have dynamic rhythm. This is a special quality of rosemaling and falls into the category of harmony in line. Good rosemaling design has a movement that carries the eye rhythmically and firmly from one area to the other. This feeling of movement and power make it typically Norwegian.

Rosemaling has planned relationship of space within the design. In rosemaling the relationship of design area to background area is of basic importance. For example, in painting Telemark style the feeling of "air" or openness should be present through the use of transparency, while in painting Hallingdal style the feeling of space comes from the openness of the designs themselves.

Rosemaling designs must have feeling. Any art can be technically fine but still look dead. Rosemaling, as a rule, had feeling, a sort of aliveness and strength that was imparted through all of its forms, particularly the scrolls and curves. Often it was due to the great variety in forms, but again it could be because of the dash and originality of the artist.

Figure 143. This linework illustrates how effectively broken lines can add interest to rosemaling. Notice how the outline of the reclining nude form on pg. 186 gains structure and life with broken lines. In the same manner stopping lines and varying their length gives vitality to rosemaling forms.

8
The Use of Rosemaling
in Contemporary Life

THE TRANSITION from the traditional farm house to the various building styles of twentieth-century houses presents an exciting challenge to today's rosemaler. This challenge can best be met by setting forth a few basic decorating principles and letting the rosemaler follow these principles along with his best judgment to achieve the proper decorative effect.

In the old days the architectural style of the houses allowed for more elaborate rosemaling. The huge beams, large fireplaces, heavy unitized furniture, and bare wood gave rooms a strength which needed the softening influence that rosemaling could give. Even curtains, which might detract from rosemaling, were often missing, in order to let as much light as possible through the windows. As a result the rosemaling could be used much more lavishly than in today's large windowed and lavishly furnished homes. The crux of the matter is that in the olden days rosemaling *was* the decoration, whereas today's homes are usually decorated with paintings, bookshelves, patterned curtains, and sofas, to name but a few of the items that are almost a standard part of the average room's decor. Under these conditions rosemaling becomes more of an *accent* than a chief decorating element. If you intend to make rosemaling the decorating pivot upon which the rest of the room turns, you must eliminate most other decorative accents such as patterned fabrics and upholstery and concentrate on emphasizing it alone. This means that you must use plain colors on the furniture and avoid silks or chintzes, which are too feminine to combine well with rosemaling. Wools and linens have the strength to complement rosemaling and are also the traditional fabrics used in Norway. Some of today's synthetics have weaves that simulate these fabrics and will do nicely, too. However, be sure to choose these fabrics in the colors that you know will appear in the painting. If the room has already been decorated, you will have to eliminate any pattern that detracts from the rosemaling and use the colors that already predominate in the room in your rosemaling.

188

A strong, simple room can handle a great deal of rosemaling, on the ceiling, the doors, or furniture panels. If you use a quantity of rosemaling in a small room, it is usually better to paint in the same general style (for example Telemark) on similar objects such as door panels. You can use a different style on a dissimilar object as long as the design fits the space and harmonizes color-wise. As mentioned previously, the old rosemalers often used two contrasting styles of painting on an important piece of furniture such as a cupboard. The major, recessed panels were sometimes painted with a symmetrical design, while the border would have a flowing design. This method can still be followed if you are careful to coordinate the colors so that the border design will be done in one or at the most, two colors of the main design.

Figure 144. The peaceful interior of a typical rural farm home in Norway today. The farm is called Spikketrå and is in the Telemark district. Copyright: © Photos Norge

Figure 145. Porch connected to the main cottage at Binkhaven. The wood-carved panels and turned supporting posts were brought from Norway. Copyright: © Photos Norge

Figure 146. Veslebur (little storehouse) and stabbur (two-story loft) at Binkhaven. Both buildings were imported from Norway. Copyright: © Photos Norge

There tend to be many more objets d'art and knick-knacks around in modern rooms than in the old Norwegian ones. In olden times everything in the home was functional, so there was very little to compete with the rosemaling decoration. Today we have more money for collecting and more space for displaying items that interest and please us. These objects reflect our personalities and give our houses a lived-in look. Small objects that have been rosemaled will fit perfectly into such a situation. However, most knick-knack articles of any type would have to be eliminated or at least put into another part of the house before any rosemaling could be used as a major decorative feature in a room.

To give some idea of the tremendous possibilities for the use of rosemaling let us now consider some of the following ideas. These suggestions are for both minor projects and ambitious ones. Try those which appeal to you, and then go a step further and think up your own special, original uses. This chapter makes no attempt to list all the possible applications of this art form.

SMALL OBJECTS

In considering the possibilities for rosemaling, a good place to start is with smaller objects. Some of these items, such as plates, bowls, and trays, are very obvious, but remember that *anything* that is wooden can be rosemaled. For instance: footstools, breadboxes, trunks, firewood boxes, children's furniture, and jewelry boxes are all satisfying to decorate and become more interesting as a result of rosemaling.

Although anything wooden *can* be painted with rosemaling there are some wooden objects that should *not* be! Choose your items with care so that you do not paint on an unattractive, poorly constructed, and poorly designed item just because it is wooden. There is no point in wasting your precious time and energy on a homely object of poor quality that no amount of work can render beautiful.

At the same time it cannot be stressed enough that you should *not* consider decorating an antique or redecorating an object that has been previously decorated unless you are really qualified to restore it. Old pieces are frequently beautiful left as they are and have a special charm that can be destroyed by painting and redecorating. Often they tell the story of a family by their marks and scars—pleasing traces all too easily destroyed.

If an article has already been decorated but the painting has faded, try using turpentine and linseed oil to clean it and restore the color. Often that is all an object needs to bring back the vividness of the colors.

The best source of the most attractive wooden items is still Norway, where you still can find craftsmanship at a high level. Plates, platters, and bowls are turned on wood lathes and sanded to a satiny finish that gives

each object a distinctly well-designed "made in Norway" look. Even more beautiful than the small items are pieces of furniture, such as wooden chests with hand-wrought iron fittings. Practical uses for chests include: a receptacle for storing blankets and clothes; a wood box for the fireplace or one converted into a tape and stereo cabinet by the simple addition of a wooden shelf. Along with trunks, other handsome pieces of wooden furniture can be imported from Norway. Hutches, corner cupboards, chairs, tables, and wall cabinets are designed in the traditional style of old Norwegian furniture but adapted to modern life. A piece of this furniture decorated with rosemaling would be a beautiful addition to any home. Many American craftsmen could duplicate such wooden furniture, but there are very few who are willing to devote the time to undertake such work.

Most local craft stores carry some inexpensive, unfinished woodenware that is fine to learn on. Once your eye is trained to see good line and judge quality, you can begin to haunt your local junk and antique shops for bargains that are appropriate to fix up and rosemale; but until that time it is best to confine your buying to inexpensive objects. In the United States one of the best sources of quality Norwegian woodenware is the Norwegian-American Museum in Decorah, Iowa, which publishes a list of the items it handles. Ordering directly from Norway may entail more delays than most people anticipate, but remember that there is a language barrier and the small outlets handcraft their items and do

Figure 149. Rosemaled wooden furniture in a shop in the Hallingdal district of Norway. Most of the painting here has been done by Nils Ellingsgard or his cousin Lars Sataøyen. This shop was a stop on the 1970 Rosemaling Tour sponsored by the Norwegian-American Museum. Copyright: © Photos Norge

not produce in mass. Also, everything is shipped via ocean freight, which in itself takes at least six weeks from loading to destination port. Experience has shown that the Husflidens* (the Norwegian handicraft outlets located throughout the country) are geared to tourists and foreign trade and are in a position to handle your order. There is no language barrier and they are more apt to answer your letters and ship objects promptly than are the smaller shops that are directed to the domestic trade. The Husflidens in Oslo and Ytre Arna are the largest stores of this kind and are usually more prompt in replying to inquiries.

EXTERIOR APPLICATIONS

Since rosemaling is essentially a form of interior decoration it has little practical application on the exterior of homes. Decorating shutters and doors is more characteristic of Swiss or Pennsylvania Dutch painting than of rosemaling. However, if you live in an area with a mild climate and have a rustic style of house you can use rosemaling to decorate certain small areas. A wooden door with moldings, an attractive mailbox, and possibly a wooden sign with your name or house number and street would be interesting items to decorate with simple scrolls and flowers.

* There are Husflidens in Skien, Kristiansand, Stavanger, Bergen, Ålesund, Trondheim, Tromsø, Bodø, Lillehammer and Ytre Arna, to name some good ones. Address inquiries to Norsk Husfliden in the town in which the outlet is located.

Figure 151. Front door painted in Hallingdal style by Margaret M. Miller. This design was adapted to fit the door panels from an original design by Nils Ellingsgard. Copyright: Margaret M. Miller

INTERIOR APPLICATIONS

The interior of a home allows for great freedom of decoration. Remember, though, the amount of rosemaling you use should depend upon your willingness to give up other accessories in the room.

Entryways

In the entry hall you may want to paint the inside of the front door. If the foyer is decorated in a rather sophisticated style, a subtle and elegant type of rosemaling would be called for. This can be achieved by painting your design all in one color, or at the most two, and outlining with a color only slightly darker than the colors you use on the design itself. In this case the design should mostly be scrolls, which are more subdued and sophisticated in appearance. The outlining should be sparse, used mainly around the major curves, with little or no detail work. On the other hand, if the foyer has no special decorative feeling it can be made cheerful and friendly by rosemaling in more vibrant colors and using a design with flowers springing from the scrolls to give it a lively appearance.

If the door is made of plain plywood you can prepare it for rosemaling simply by using half-round molding to create panels. Remember that whenever you paint on a fairly large area the painting *must* be contained by either molding or some kind of paneling. Another way to achieve a paneled effect is to buy wide, white pine boards at a lumber yard. Have the rectangle cut in an attractive decorative shape and routed around the edges. Next paint the door itself a color that will contrast interestingly with the walls. Paint the routed edges a contrasting color and the face of the panels themselves still another color. Then decorate the panels with rosemaling. When they are dry, screw the panels to the door. You will be amazed at the decorative impact it will have as an accent for the entire house. The panels alone will give the door a much more finished look. One excellent advanage to this method is that you can work on a table and not on the door itself. Both these methods of creating panels can be used on the outside of the door, too, as long as the weather is not severe.

The old Norwegian rosemalers sometimes depicted scenes that interested them. Special family events, such as weddings, or the arrival of an important person were considered of sufficient interest to be painted on the center of a panel, surrounded by the scrolls and flowers of rosemaling. This type of figure motif was even more characteristic of the *blomstermåling* (flower painting) that flourished in nearby Sweden at about this same period. This type of design would be interesting for a door panel.

Frequently there will be a credenza, or narrow cabinet with a mirror hanging over it, in an entry way. Consider painting the credenza and

mirror frame to match. Some foyers have space for a bench where people can sit down to pull off their boots. The back rest on such a bench is an interesting place for rosemaling. A wooden umbrella stand is still another piece of foyer furniture that can be decorated.

Kitchens

The kitchen, because it is so much the personal domain of the house-wife, is often the room most adaptable to rosemaling and the greatest joy to decorate. You may want to do the cabinets right away, but it will be better if you wait until your skill with design, brush, and color has developed more strength. If you paint numerous cabinet doors, keep your designs simple and your colors restricted to two or three so as not to overwhelm your kitchen with a vibrant display of color and a pro-fusion of blooms and curves.

Painting on kitchen cabinets should, as with any flat surface, be enclosed by molding or done on panels that are recessed below or raised above the surface level of the cabinet door. The purpose of this is to restrict the design area, much the same as a mat encloses a painting. It would not do to let the design wander to the edges of the cabinet doors. If your cabinets are completely flat and you feel that you cannot afford molding or panels, you can paint enclosing lines to simulate molding.

To paint these enclosing lines, carefully draw the outline you would have if you were applying a molding, using a ruler and pencil. Be sure to draw the inside and outside edges of the banding and check to see that all widths are even. Then simply paint the molding on with the color of your choice. A molding brush such as the one mentioned in Chapter 3 works well for this purpose, or a round brush of the appropri-ate size, usually made of camel's hair, which is less expensive. If you cannot find the color you want in a commercial brand, mix the desired color with your oil paints just as you do for rosemaling. The color will usually take slightly longer to dry because of the quantity of oil used in mixing, but you will achieve the desired effect. To give the painted molding more depth and dimension, paint a thin line along the entire inside of the molding in a darker or lighter color than the one you used for the molding itself.

A major problem in most kitchens is choosing the kind of treatment for the windows that will admit a maximum of light. In many kitchens a decorated cornice made of plywood that would either fit across the top of the windows or frame them on three sides would be a good solution. After giving the cornices the base coats, you can decorate them with

Figure 152. Door in Mil-ler's Clothing House, Stur-geon Bay, Wisconsin. Painted in Telemark style by Margaret M. Miller and antiqued with raw umber. Raised moldings have made frames on the flat door. Copyright: Harmann Stu-dios

rosemaling and have a stunning effect. You can add privacy and soften the effect by using simple cafe style curtains or you can add nighttime privacy with louvered shutters that will fold back during the day. The same approach can apply equally well to bedrooms, family rooms, and bathrooms. With this much rosemaling around the windows it would probably be too overwhelming to rosemale kitchen cupboards too; however, they can be treated with antiquing or glazing (see Chapter 7). Decide what will be most attractive in your particular situation. One other method for handling windows would be to use the solid style shutters only and decorate the inset area in each panel.

Living Areas

The dining room, living room, and family room are usually excellent to decorate or paint with rosemaling because they are large rooms and are likely to have beamed ceilings; these automatically give a natural area for rosemaling. If you are trying to decide whether to paint the ceiling itself or the beams, consider these factors. Do not paint areas that are hard to see. For instance, if the ceiling is very high, rosemaling on the sides of beams will be almost impossible to see and the painting will become too small to appreciate at a distance. The place to paint in such a case would be between the beams, on the ceiling itself. The painting would thus be big enough to see easily and the height of the ceiling would allow the room to carry the large amount of decoration. Conversely, beams in a rather low ceiling look especially well when painted on both sides, but if the ceiling were painted the decoration could overwhelm the room and cause it to look lower. The exception to this rule is that a low ceiling can be painted if it is not large or in a living area. You must be more careful in a room used every day, but entryways, bathrooms, and small bedrooms can usually have their ceilings decorated. If you have a room with a beamed ceiling that slopes slightly, such as a dormer bedroom, it would be appropriate to paint both the sides and the bottoms of the beams.

Contemporary furniture usually derives its beauty from simplicity of line and the quality of its wood, so you would not want to rosemal it. However, if your home is modern and you want to incorporate some major rosemaling, you can do so by painting directly on the wall and enclosing the design with molding, or you can paint large panels and apply them to the walls. Thus the rosemaling will look more like a large, framed painting, and because it is dramatic it will blend well with the contemporary wood and add color and pattern.

Figure 153. Kitchen at Binkhaven Nord with modern rosemaling by Sigmund Aarseth. The colors in the designs are bright blue, black, and white. Copyright: © Photos Norge

Figure 154. Closeup of the beams downstairs in the main cottage at Binkhaven. Copyright: © Photos Norge

A treatment that is quite easy to do and really brightens a room is to rosemal a border just below where the walls join the ceiling. This is particularly attractive in halls, dining rooms, bathrooms, or dens. Decide how wide you want the border by experimenting with different width bands of paper which you can fasten to the wall temporarily with scotch tape. You will find that the higher the ceiling, the wider the border must be. Do not put the design right next to the ceiling but rather several inches below it, so you will have room for color bandings to simulate moldings between the design and the ceiling and keep an appropriate space relationship. Then carefully measure the width of the border you have decided on all around the walls and rule them lightly in chalk. Paint your design within these margins, preferably using a repetitive pattern. Again, you will have to restrict your colors to two or three and use less outlining than usual.

MISCELLANEOUS APPLICATIONS

At this point it would be well to mention that rosemaling is not only creatively satisfying and beautifully decorative, it is relatively inexpensive. After your initial outlay for paint and brushes you can enhance the appearance of your entire house with your skill and make it much more personal in the process.

Figure 155. Rosemaler Sigmund Aarseth painted this door panel at Binkhaven more in the style of his native area of Valdres in Norway. Copyright: © Photos Norge

Do not be afraid to do your rosemaling in the form of a painting to be framed like a picture and hung on the walls. Cut masonite panels to a size that will fit inside a standard picture frame. You can determine these sizes by checking at your local art supply store. After you have painted a design you feel will be suitable as a picture, simply frame it and hang it up. Remember that the plainer the frame, the more attention will be given the painting. Norwegian designs with figures in them are particularly suitable for this use. Or a rosemaled panel can be enclosed with molding and mounted on a door.

A nursery or child's room has endless possibilities for rosemaling. Besides painting on bureaus, doors, cribs, bunks, and headboards you can paint a gay picture right on the wall with a floral and scroll frame around it. Any child will be delighted with a footlocker or trunk painted for use as a toy box, and it may make him more interested in putting his toys away. Put the child's name or initials and the date of his birth on the items you paint for him so that he will feel they are something that really belong to him. Most children appreciate and take better care of furnishings that have been personalized for them.

One last possibility should be considered before you start using your own imagination to apply the countless variations of rosemaling that have not been touched on. Traditionally, the designs embroidered on the famous *bunad*, or costumes worn by women for special occasions, were closely related to the rosemaling of each district. This same embroidery

Figure 156. This mantel at "Pheasant Farm," the home of the Dean Maddens in Decatur, Illinois, was carved by Norwegian woodcarver Ole Bismo and painted by Nils Ellingsgard. The shading is a soft blue. Copyright: © Photos Norge

Figure 157. Photo of the Telemark rosemaling by Sigmund Aarseth in a bedroom in his home in Valdres, Norway. Observe the light lasur treatment which shows up in the closeup of one of the panels. Copyright: Kolbein Dahle

of rosemaling designs can be adapted to furnishings as well. Anyone who is talented with a needle will be able to adapt the lovely designs to bedspreads, pictures, and pillow covers in much the same way that crewel work is used. Some women have even hooked rosemaling patterns into rugs. One note of caution only: stick with the colors and fabrics of the Norwegian folk arts. Work with wool-on-wool or wool-on-linen and use the type of hues described in the color chapter.

It is now apparent that rosemaling has swung full circle and is as relevant and beautiful today as it was centuries ago in Norway. Thus the spirit of the decorative artists of the eighteenth century continues to flourish in America as well as on its native soil. Few nations can claim such a vital continuity of tradition as Norway: a heritage that has now survived industrial and artistic upheavals to claim a place in modern society.

Since a society never remains static it is hoped that contemporary rosemalers will continue to grow and to develop their own styles. A revival of certain fine techniques that have nearly been lost would contribute to this growth. The discipline of rosemaling, the freedom of brush strokes, the skillful use of transparent technique, and the striving of each individual artist for originality will automatically channel themselves into development. These tools may then be used experimentally to push rosemaling into new design areas without sacrificing any of the vividness of color, line, and craftsmanship that characterize the art.

REFERENCES

Randi Asker, *Rose-Painting in Norway;* Dreyers Forlag; Oslo 1967.

Gunnar Bugge and Christian Norberg-Schulz; *Stav og Laft i Norge;* Norske Arkitekters Landsforbund; Oslo 1969.

Roar Hauglid; *Norwegian Stave Churches;* Dreyers Forlag; Oslo 1970.

Kristian Kildal; *Vaar Gamle Folkekunst;* Grondahl & Sons Forlag; Oslo 1961.

Tre Tryckare; *The Viking;* International Book Society, Cagner & Co. 1966.

Øystein Vesaas; *Rosemaling in the Telemark;* Mittet & Co. A/S; Oslo 1955.

Janice S. Stewart, *The Folk Arts of Norway,* Dover Publications, Ihc.; New York 1972.

Paintings from the Stave Churches; Unesco World Art Series; Milan 1955.

John Midgaard, *A Brief History of Norway;* Johan Grundt Tanum Forlag, Oslo.

Ruth Morton, Hilda Geuther, Virginia Guthrie, *The Home—Its Furnishings and Equipment;* Chapter 10; McGraw-Hill, Inc.; New York 1970.

Ethel Kvalheim, *How to Do Rosemaling;* Ethel Kvalheim, Stoughton, Wis.; 1970.

Arthur L. Guptill; *Color In Sketching and Rendering;* Reinhold Publishing Company; New York 1949.

Iona Plath, *Decorative Arts of Sweden;* Charles Scribner's Sons; New York 1948.

Index